DONORS
ARE PEOPLE TOO

MANAGING RELATIONSHIPS
WITH YOUR MINISTRY'S
MAJOR CONTRIBUTORS

by Timothy Smith

FOREWORD BY E. DALE BERKEY, PH.D.

Donors Are People Too

Managing Relationships With Your Ministry's Major Contributors

by Timothy Smith

Foreword by E. Dale Berkey, Ph.D.

BERKEY BRENDEL SHELINE
Ministry Development Specialists
60 Shiawassee, Suite G • Akron, OH 44333
voice (330) 867-5224 • fax (330) 869-5607
email servant@servantheart.com
www.servantheart.com

Table of Contents

Not Created Equal

We've had the joy of helping ministries for nearly three decades. It's a privilege to see people supporting ministry organizations the world over through the strategies that God has helped us to develop.

Certainly the vast majority of donors to ministry organizations still participate through "mass media" — the mail, the telephone, the Internet. No Christian charity in the world has enough staff members to sit down with every donor personally and form a personal relationship. But over time, certain donors emerge as major players. They give more than the average individual, signaling their higher level of interest in the cause — and their interest in a closer relationship with the ministry organization.

How should the ministry organization respond to these major donors? Is it right to give them any extraordinary attention at all?

Some quote chapter 2 of the book of James to argue against any special focus on major donors at all. This, sadly, misses the point of that biblical passage. James warns against treating the rich well to the detriment of the poor. A healthy ministry will invest itself in all of its donors to the full extent of the organization's capacity. With unlimited resources, the organization could treat every donor like a major donor. But with limited resources, the organization must invest in each donor according to the donor's expressed level of interest in the mission of the organization. This is not cynical; it is good, practical stewardship.

We instinctively obey the same principle of life in our personal friendships: I do not invest the same amount of time, energy, attention, and affection in every person I know. I focus my life-resources proportionately, based on the relationships that mean the most to me. How did I decide which relationships mean the most to me? Certain individuals emerged and, by whatever means, demonstrated a higher level of interest: my spouse, my son, my parents, my close friends, my partners and team, and so forth.

The book of James bans ugly-spirited, self-serving favoritism which ignores the poor. Accordingly, a Christian ministry should not focus exclusively on major donors, ignoring lower-level donors. Indeed, our agency's 1999 book *Seven Deadly Diseases of Ministry Marketing* is designed to help ministries communicate with and invest in the multitudes of "average" donors. But as major donors step out from the crowd and indicate through their higher levels of giving that they want to be more deeply involved in your ministry's work, you need to respond appropriately.

So in the pages that follow, we offer insights into the care and keeping of major donors — approaches which we have found to be biblically sound, cost-efficient, and spiritually effective.

Our agency is proud to have Tim Smith as our specialist in major donor relationships. Tim has a rich background in pastoral ministry and years of successful experience in dealing with major donors. But he did not spring from the earth fully formed; he has learned a lot "the hard way." One of his best qualities is his willingness to confront his own failures and learn from them, to reveal his experiences and share wisdom through them. His candor is refreshing, and his insights are valuable. (I am also grateful for the contribution of Doug Brendel, who co-founded the agency with me; Doug wordsmithed the book for Tim.)

We would welcome the opportunity to interact with you

about the major donor aspect of your ministry organization, for the sake of advancing the cause of Christ through your unique God-given mission. Please feel free to contact us.

E. Dale Berkey, Ph.D., President
BERKEY BRENDEL SHELINE
servant@servantheart.com

CHAPTER 1

Something Wrong With Whom?

Fun? Absolutely. When I was a youth pastor, our program was awesome.

Intense? Oh, yeah. So much going on, you could hardly catch your breath. The kids *loved* it.

Learning? No question about it. Bible study was never so cool. Scriptures a-plenty, dude.

Results? Powerful. Teens having phenomenal altar-call-type encounters with God, repenting of sin and committing their lives to Him.

Long-term value? Uh ... well ... let's go back and talk some more about all that fun and all that learning.

The truth was, every year as I looked back over another 12 months of ministry, I was uneasy. The teens in my group were all hyped up about the ministry, and they would respond powerfully at come-to-Jesus time. But then the passion would drain away. The mark of Christ on their lives would fade. I would have to come up with something bigger and better for the next programming cycle. And the same kids would make the same commitments the next year (or in some cases the next month).

And for what ultimate purpose? The redundancy of my ministry was discouraging. If permanent life-change wasn't happening, why was I working in ministry at all?

Obviously, I said to myself, *there is something wrong with kids today.*

Disillusioned but still deeply committed to God's work, I moved into ministry to young couples. By now I was attending seminary, and I brought to this new endeavor a passion for the Scriptures. Every week I constructed fascinating 40-minute Scripture talks, enriched with the historical and cultural context of the passage, insights into the original Greek or Hebrew, and presented with comedy and other entertaining devices for a memorable learning experience. Our church was big, and my ministry was successful, so we had some 200 young adults in our group. I was having a blast.

If permanent life-change wasn't happening, why was I working in ministry at all?

One Sunday a sharp young friend of mine, Tim Martin, came up to me after the class. "Wow, Tim, I could tell you really studied this week!" he said.

I beamed. "Thanks," I replied.

"But you know what?" he went on. "I can't think of one thing you said this morning that I can take home with me, or that Betsy and I can use this week in our marriage."

At first I thought he must be joking. "Gee, thanks, Tim," I smirked. But he didn't back down, didn't go on to the punchline. He was dead serious.

I fumed on the way home. *Obviously,* I said to myself,

there's something wrong with Tim Martin.

Can you believe what Tim Martin said to me after class today? I groused to my wife. I quoted the offending comment.

"He's right," she replied with a shrug.

Shocked and appalled, I skulked into the house. Now I was ready to yell at the kids and kick the dog. *Obviously*, I said to myself, *there's something wrong with my wife!*

The light was beginning to dawn.

The teens in my youth group loved the program, but there wasn't much long-term impact happening in their lives. They didn't sense that I was really there for *them*; I was there to produce a program. The young couples in my group at church were dazzled by my performance, but they weren't taking much of practical value home with them. They didn't sense that I was there to care for them; they sensed that I was there to impress them.

> *"I can't think of one thing you said this morning that I can take home with me, or that Betsy and I can use this week in our marriage."*

The uncomfortable truth was gradually sinking in. The problem wasn't with the kids. The problem wasn't with the couples. The problem wasn't with Tim Martin, or my wife, or my kids, or my dog.

The problem was with me.

I was doing programs — I was performing — I was shooting at people like targets, trying to hit a bull's-eye and get the desired response. But I wasn't bringing something of real value into their lives.

I wasn't really *ministering*.

As I asked God to show me what I needed to see, I began

to see that room full of people as *individuals*. Instead of some kind of "audience" in which I was trying to generate a certain "response function," I began to see *people* ... people with needs, people with a longing for warm, nurturing relationships. Each one was a person in need of a friend, someone to walk life's road with, to confide in, to sort things out with, to be challenged by and comforted by, to pray with, to call at a crisis point in the middle of the night.

Instead of some kind of "audience" in which I was trying to generate a certain "response function," I began to see people ...

I realized that I could never establish a deep, intimate, soul-enriching friendship like that with all 200 people in that class. I might be able to develop that kind of relationship with six or eight, though, and each of them might be able to do likewise with another six or eight — and so on, until the entire group was not just experiencing "ministry programs," but living in true "community."

The turning of that corner dramatically changed my life and ministry. Sure, I could get bursts of response from teens or young couples or whatever "audience" happened to be in my line of fire; I was persuasive and I was promoting "God's work." But those bursts of response were not nearly as productive in the lives of those individuals as a genuine, caring relationship could be.

Those bursts of response were not nearly as productive in the lives of those individuals as a genuine, caring relationship could be.

Some years later, God led me into the rather unusual realm of major donor ministry. A new ministry was being

4

established in the Phoenix area, and I was responsible for raising a quarter million dollars in a year — starting virtually from scratch, with practically no donor base. I blitzed the entire metropolitan area, cramming my Day-Timer with appointments, talking to as many people as I could, shooting my standard speech at each prospect almost like a desperate man with a gun. *Can you give a thousand dollars? Can you give a thousand dollars?* No sense of relationship. No getting to know the person, to assess whether such a request were appropriate. Just asking, asking, asking.

At campaign's end, I sat exhausted in a restaurant, staring sullenly at nearly 300 file cards, each one representing a contact. I had made the goal — but I knew there was no way I could ever do this again. The ministry would need another quarter million dollars for another stage of its growth, but I could not keep this kind of pace. It was grueling physically, it was utterly unsatisfying emotionally — and I had contributed little or nothing to

Something inside told me, this was no way to treat people.

the lives of the 250 people who had contributed. Something inside told me, this was no way to treat people. Something within me wanted to see them as real people, not as financial assets to the corporation.

Gradually, the fog lifted. I remembered the youth group. I remembered the young couples. I remembered that darn Tim Martin. And I realized that I needed to approach major donor ministry as *ministry*, not fundraising. I needed to make friends, care for individuals, invest in relationships. I certainly couldn't develop 300 authentic friendships in a year — but I might be able to focus on 50 or 60 or possibly 75 of those individuals over time ... get to know them, contribute to their lives, and see what God would do in them and through them for the sake of the ministry's mission.

Fried with fatigue, I drew a line in the sand of my life. Even if I never achieved another fundraising goal in my life, I couldn't keep living like this. But if God was really leading me, then I could trust Him to provide the funding — through *realer* relationships with *fewer* people.

Authentic relationships with major donors produce an array of benefits.

As I have discovered in the years since then, authentic relationships with major donors produce an array of benefits: I am less likely to burn out. The donor doesn't burn out. The donor actually tends to give more, and more joyfully, and for a longer period of time. Most importantly, through my ministry to that individual, the organization is pouring something of lasting value into that person's life. This is an approach of both quantitative and qualitative value.

Follow the trail of someone's money over time, and you'll find the real object of their passion. A man may give a gift in response to a request, but without a passion for that ministry, he will soon find a way to avoid future requests. My goal in major donor ministry is to grow *friends*, to minister truly and deeply to individuals, whether they ever give again or not. *We become stakeholders in each other's lives.* But because of my passion for my organization's mission, and

We become stakeholders in each other's lives.

because of the deepening relationship between that donor and me, it's almost inevitable that the donor will grow more committed to the ministry I'm involved with. His giving, then, will be a by-product of that commitment.

And at the end of the day, I will lay my head on my pillow with a deep sense of satisfaction, not just because someone contributed to my ministry, but because I contributed. I didn't just represent a ministry; I *did* ministry.

CHAPTER 2

The Donor, Not the Donation

It is easy to think about the *gift* as the end-product of major donor ministry. But the gift is only a *by-product*. The end-product of major donor ministry is the *donor* ... a friend who is growing in Christ, thriving spiritually, and joyfully committed to being used by God in the mission of your ministry organization. In fact, this "end-product" is actually an *ongoing* product.

The end-product of major donor ministry is the donor.

Down through the years, as I have lived and taught this approach to major donor ministry, some of my colleagues in ministry have recoiled. It's too "pastoral," they feel, not "systematic" enough. The fact is, I am a very systematic person. I like to make a plan, work the plan, evaluate the plan. But my plans and systems for extracting gifts from major donors did more to wear me down than to build up the ministry — and they certainly did nothing for the donors themselves. In the pages that follow, we'll walk through a system for ministry to major donors. But at the heart of this system is a truth that it took me years to understand: *It is never about the donation; it is always about the donor.*

Any healthy system, then, must also be about donors, not about donations. When I began serving in fundraising ministry, my first "database" was a small stack of 3-by-5 cards and one of those fat ink pens with four colors instead of just one. I began with a rubber band around the cards, then graduated to a little recipe box. Eventually I needed a file box, then two file boxes. I kept everything in the trunk of my car; thank God it was never stolen, because there was no backup!

The four-color pen helped me keep track of the donors. Anything written on a card in red meant there was trouble: the donor was unhappy with the organization, or was having trouble at home or work. Blue was for warm, fuzzy relational stuff. Green meant money: the donor had given something. And black was for everything else. I came to see each 3-by-5 card as a human being, and the color-coded notes simply held in place the personal details that my memory wouldn't.

The ministry was too broke to give me a computer or the privacy of an office; I had a desk and a phone in a cubicle. (If a mailing needed to be produced, I wrote it, duplicated it, folded it, stuffed the envelopes, licked the stamps, and dropped everything in the mailbox.) My office of choice was the Coffee Plantation, a little café in Tempe, Arizona. I would sit at an outdoor table, spread out my file cards for the day, review the color-coded notes, and start calling people on my primitive early-model cell phone.

On a January afternoon as I sat in my usual spot, I began to realize something about the donors to my ministry organization. Even though by now I had worked hard to build relationships with my donors, 27 of them had not given a year-end gift. I had met with them, I asked them for a gift, they had committed to give a gift. But they hadn't actually given the gift. For the remainder of that afternoon, I sat at that little table and wrote notes. Each of the 27 donors received a personal note thanking them for their commitment to our work. I told them of the great year-end campaign we had just completed. I promised a phone call in the near future. But I didn't mention their failure to give the gift they had promised to give.

But when we care more about the donor than the donation, donations tend to follow.

Within ten days, 18 of those 27 donors sent a gift. In some cases they included an apology for having forgotten their pledge. (It turned out to be the biggest January for income that the organization had ever had.)

Certainly it's not possible to raise money without asking for money — and in these pages we will walk through the specifics of how that happens. But when we care more about the donor than the donation, donations tend to follow. My 27 donors knew me; I knew them. Our relationship was intimate enough, our lives were integrated enough, that I might call one of them about our sons' Little League schedule and it would jog his memory of our conversation about the fundraising campaign. Yes, they were my "donors," but they were people too ... and they sensed that I was relating to them as people, as friends. Gifts to my ministry organization followed naturally, not as the result of a "system."

A young man called out to me across the lobby of our church after the service one Sunday morning. "Tim! Tim! I need to talk to you!" He made his way through the crowd and was out of breath when he got to me. Taking me by the elbow, he pointed out a new attendee.

"His name is Jim," he said breathlessly, "and he has a lot of money. You need to talk to him."

I just smiled. My young friend didn't get it. He pictured me as a fundraising machine and donors as fund-*giving* machines. But to pursue donations with that philosophy is exhausting and demeaning. Having tried it in the early days, knowing no better, I had found myself in a career death spiral, and deeply unhappy. I wasn't going to talk to the newcomer at our church because he had a lot of money; I was going to welcome him as a new friend.

If we don't see ministry to the donor as our higher calling, our donors are destined to be mere objects.

Donors need *relationship* and *ministry* far more than I need their money. If we don't see *ministry to the donor* as our higher calling, our donors are destined to be mere objects in our lives and in our organizations — and the connection between us and them will be sadly unsatisfying.

As I speak and teach on this subject at conferences across the country, one of the most frequently asked questions is about trust: "How do donors learn to trust your friendship when they know what you do for a living — and that you really want them to give to your organization?"

To answer the question, we can look at any healthy friendship and inspect the dynamics of the interaction between the two parties. What do they talk about? What do they receive from each other? What do they require of each other? In a healthy friendship, it's not all about just one friend or the other. The interaction isn't all about one guy's job, or one person's family issues.

I set out to make a friend. I don't do that by talking all about myself, my work, my ministry, my need. Eventually, that friend may become a donor to my organization. But by that time, I have already had the privilege of entering into a friendship, a valuable relationship, with that person; I have already *ministered* to that person relationally.

Oh sure, but from the very beginning, that person knows your ultimate intention. I hear this objection frequently. Someone whose ministry focuses on major donors is often put in the position of being introduced to a prospective donor for the express purpose of acquiring a contribution. It's an essentially "artificial" way to meet a new friend, isn't it! But consider the analogy of two next-door neighbors. Over time, they become friends. They come to know each other's families, they swap stories about their jobs. The day comes when one gets in a bind and needs to borrow the other's lawnmower or ask for emergency babysitting or whatever. I can get into a schedule crisis and ask my next-door neighbor to give me a lift to the airport — and why him? I have chosen him to request help from, simply because of an accident of location: we happened to buy houses next to each other. Our relationship was born of artificial means. But I invested in the relationship anyway; he came to realize that I cared about him, even though he had little or no choice in the matter of my coming into his life. He doesn't mistrust me for that. The fact is that many of our relationships in life begin in this "artificial" way — they start out based on one "reason for being," but morph into something else.

In the same way, when I call on a stranger because they have been recommended as a potential donor to my ministry, I certainly start out by introducing myself and my organization, and there's no question that I hope they'll get involved. But in the course of my talks with that individual, I will focus far more on that person — getting to know him, discovering him for his own sake, not his money's sake — than on myself or my quest.

I want to know if there's a way I can invest, be helpful, pray, love.

I go into that relationship — contrived as it may be from the very beginning — with one primary question in mind: Is there a way I can minister to this person? I want to know if there's a way I can invest, be helpful, pray, love.

It's possible that the person may give to my organization eventually, but that will be a by-product, not the end-product, of the relationship.

Some of my closest friends today are people I first met years ago in the strange circumstances of a fundraising appointment or the "artificial" environment of a fundraising event. We happened to find that we had a lot in common; we got along especially well. Over the years, these wonderful people have invested at least as much in me as I have in them. Some have contributed enormously to the ministry organizations I've represented. Coincidentally, my "best donors" are the people I happen to relate to the best. But each friendship endures on its own, irrespective of financial contributions to any ministry.

The truth is that only a slender percentage of my life and work involves asking for money.

When I meet with major donors or prospects, I focus on them, not me. I focus on their lives, not my ministry organization's next challenge. And I certainly don't ask them for money every time I get together with them. The myth of the "major donor solicitor" (a horrible

14

term but one which is widely used anyway) is that every conversation is either a "setting up" for a "sale" — or the "close" of the "sale." If this were true, it would be a grim kind of work indeed. The truth is that only a slender percentage of my life and work involves asking for money. I spend much more time listening to and ministering to donors!

CHAPTER 3

That One in a Million

Many ministry organizations have a backward view of major donors. They are waiting, hoping, praying, searching for that "one in a million" donor — that one with millions! So they organize their major donor ministry as a kind of radar-sensitive search-and-destroy effort. This is the organizational equivalent of playing the lottery. Not only are the odds very long, but the organization's trust is misplaced. God has ordained that most ministries will be nourished by many donors, not just one or two donors; this enables more people to experience the blessing of giving. To avoid acquiring donors implies that giving to God's work is unpleasant or unhealthy; the opposite is true.

Moreover, a ministry which *finds* that "one in a million" will often struggle with an unintended side-effect: misplaced trust. I worked with a youth-oriented

> *God has ordained that most ministries will be nourished by many donors, not just one or two donors.*

ministry in the South whose board chairman routinely provided a massive contribution at year's end to make up any lingering budget deficit. He was, to put it in common terms, their "sugar daddy" — their one in a million. The leaders of the ministry would visit him every autumn, explain the estimated shortfall, and receive a donation. At first he was asked for, and he gave, $60,000. But by the time I began working with the group, he was writing checks for $300,000 or more each year.

I consulted with the group for two years. I recommended strongly that they mount a serious effort to build relationships with other major donors. The management team resisted. I sensed that they knew they could count on the chairman, so there was no pressure to do anything differently.

One day the chairman called me personally. He wanted to meet with me privately, apart from the ministry staff — something which had never happened on my previous visits. When I arrived, his business manager was on hand.

"These guys believe I'm the answer to all their problems," the chairman said, referring to the management team of the ministry. "Every year they count on me to bail them out. I don't believe they're working hard enough to find other donors."

I agreed. I had said virtually the same words to the management team on numerous occasions.

"How do I break them of this habit?" the chairman asked.

"It's easy," I shrugged. "Don't give."

The chairman and the business manager both sat up.

"You've enabled this pattern," I continued. "They won't work hard. I've been on them about this for months."

I recited how many days a year they had contracted for my consultations, and how much they were spending in fees and expenses. "They're paying a significant amount of money each year, and all they do is argue with me," I told him. "I don't mind a good argument, but I hate to see the ministry spending serious resources just to argue. You can argue for free."

"Should I really stop giving?" the chairman asked. "That will put them in desperate shape financially."

"You're not going to let them go under," I replied. "You're just going to get their attention."

A few days later, the ministry's managers indeed visited the chairman. They told him about their shortfall. And the chairman began his response with four deadly words: "Tim has counseled me...."

Finding that "one in a million" had shifted the leaders' trust away from God and onto an individual.

Livid, the ministry's leaders fired me — and spent six weeks scrambling to meet their end-of-year budget.

About three months later, the chairman called me again.

"That was a terrible, terrible time," he said.

"Yeah, tell me about it," I grumbled.

"But it really changed things," he continued. "It really helped. Now they're realizing they can't depend on one guy."

By the end of the next year, that organization had five donors giving major gifts like the chairman of the board — and the chairman himself was giving again. Finding that "one in a million" had shifted the leaders' trust away from God and onto an individual. It had also made the organization vulnerable to the whim of the one. Now the ministry was getting healthier, spiritually and financially.

Some organizations isolate "one in a million" but discover — sometimes too late — that the huge donations can come with serious strings attached. The donor wants to steer the organization; the donor wants to shift the mission; the donor

19

wants veto power over this or that aspect of the operation.

It's crucial that a ministry organization keep its trust fixed strongly and exclusively on God. The year 2000, with its run-up of the market, led to an unusually high level of giving to charities by stockholders seeking to avoid tax problems. Ministries took in a huge volume of stocks. Many fixated greedily on the new assets, shifting their trust to their new stock portfolios and the donors who delivered them.

Diversifying income sources is good financial stewardship and good spiritual stewardship.

But too many donors went out of business after September 11 the following year. Many ministry organizations were sorely disappointed — and some were severely damaged.

Our ministries need diverse sources of income. It's healthier. Diversity is safer financially and spiritually. It helps us keep our trust focused on God. And it's less likely that we'll suffer a massive financial setback. Diversifying income sources is good financial stewardship and good spiritual stewardship.

* * *

In our ministry organizations, likewise, we need to adjust our aspirations. We need to aspire to ministry, not money. The fact is, there are probably several major donors lurking in the organization's current database. If the organization will commit resources — which means staff members — to seeking out the most generous donors and establishing *friendships* with them, some number of major donors will almost certainly emerge from those relationships. But of equal importance,

We need to aspire to ministry, not money.

the organization will have *ministered* en route, in a very real and personal way, and in a valuable and important way.

I have heard the leaders of innumerable ministry organizations claim that their financial need is too great for such an approach. The investment of time, money, staff, and other resources in a long-term relational method is not feasible, they say. In many cases they have established a statistical grid and can tell me with certainty that X number of "cold calls" to prospects generates "Y" number of contributions at "Z" average dollars per gift. They drive their marketing operation by the numbers.

They have established a statistical grid and can tell me with certainty that X number of "cold calls" to prospects generates "Y" number of contributions at "Z" average dollars per gift.

But I observe a certain weakness in organizations with this view. Donors give below their capacity. They drift away with relative ease. They are easily drawn off because they are not being nourished by the ministry organization.

I have come to believe that *the strongest ministries in the next several years will be ministries with a long-term commitment to building real relationships with donors, and a true desire to have authentic ministry in those individuals' lives.*

When I pulled up short and took my 300 file cards and began asking God to help me form real friendships with as many as possible, I eventually moved into closer relationships with about 60 of those donors. Within another 18 months, those 60 donors were contributing more money to our ministry than the 300 had. They were intensely committed to the cause, deeply engaged. They were focused on the future of the work.

21

The ministry was a higher priority in their lives than it had ever been before. They counted themselves not as "donors" but as *stakeholders*, people whom God had led to this ministry for this time and for this cause: the financial undergirding of the work.

Money is not an off-limits subject; Jesus talked about money a lot.

Some wrongly believe we never talk about money with a donor. We certainly do! One of the greatest joys I experience as a ministry-based fundraiser is seeing a donor learn to love giving the way God designed us to give. I love to see the light go on in the eyes of a donor, as they come to realize that they have been enabled to exercise a God-given gift in extra measure. It's a delight to teach and lead an individual into a deeper understanding of the extraordinary role they have the potential to play in God's kingdom.

Money is not an off-limits subject; Jesus talked about money a lot. To communicate the biblical truths of good stewardship to major donors and prospects is one of the most important, and most fulfilling, keys of major donor ministry. We talk about money in the context of God's design, and we do so with a primary desire to help that individual grow in God — not with a primary desire to extract a million-dollar donation.

I have come to think of major donor ministry as mostly about ministry, and only tangentially about major donors. I call on those of us in major donor ministry to throw ourselves into the lives of donors at a deep level. If we are fulfilling our calling in Christ, we will find ourselves becoming confidant and friend, mentor and teacher.

CHAPTER 4

Can I Afford to Do This?

Fundraising is ministry — or, to be more accurate, it *should* be. Fundraising among major donors is a particular type of *ministry*, not just a complication of specialized strategies.

An idealist might complain that such personal attention should be given to donors at random, not only to those giving large amounts of money to the cause. This, however, would be unwise stewardship of the organization's resources. To spend staff time in such a "scattershot" approach would result in financial loss for the ministry. But perhaps even more significantly, larger donors are signaling their desire to be more involved; a highly personal investment of resources into that person is the appropriate response to that signal.

Fundraising among major donors is a particular type of ministry, not just a complication of specialized strategies.

We must keep in mind our responsibility as stewards of the resources entrusted to our ministries. Every day as a fundraiser, I have to make decisions regarding the use of funds being invested in my work within the organization. I must be true to God and true to the donors who have already given in order to pay my salary. I must protect the gifts they give, and fulfill the intent that drove the contribution. Stewardship is ultimately practical: Can my organization afford to have me spending time in building a relationship that doesn't have the potential to produce significant results? No. I need to focus my relationship-building and fundraising efforts on large donors because to do otherwise will undermine the work to which God has called us all.

Can my organization afford to have me spending time in building a relationship that doesn't have the potential to produce significant results?

I have been, at times, more egalitarian in my work with donors — sometimes by accident. A very wealthy couple had contributed several thousand dollars to my organization, and they agreed to open their fabulous home for our ministry's leadership to meet a number of their business contacts from around the community and share the vision of the ministry. Clearly these friends of theirs would be in the same financial stratosphere.

At this gathering I met a man I'll call Vic. The hosts had told me they didn't know him well, but they saw him at most of the functions they attended, so they assumed he was quite well off. Vic turned out to be quite interested in the work of our ministry. Over the course of the next several weeks, I spent a lot of time with him: dinner, golf outings, a vision tour of our organization's facilities. I called him repeatedly, he assured me he wanted to give to our ministry, and more than once, I asked him for the gift he had promised.

Finally it arrived in the mail. Inside a plain envelope was a single ten-dollar bill.

Ten dollars! I felt like I had robbed our ministry of the several hundred dollars I had spent in pursuit of this guy. I had cost our ministry an awful lot of money by investing as I had. Certainly Vic enjoyed all the attention I gave him. He benefited from it. But he did not have the capacity to help our ministry. And along the way, who could blame him for wondering, "How can they spend so much money when I give so little?" The correct answer: We can't.

On the other hand, relationships cultivated with higher-capacity donors can open the door for a lifetime of joyful and generous giving. I recall the year I spent shooting one-thousand-dollar requests in my first fundraising ministry. One man gave me the requested one-thousand-dollar contribution; later I read in the newspaper about his vast real estate holdings. *Hmm, he probably could have given more*, I said to myself. But I had never entered into relationship with him, never made an effort to get to know him and discover his passion for ministry. I had probably cost my ministry many thousands of dollars in lost contribution.

Relationships cultivated with higher-capacity donors can open the door for a lifetime of joyful and generous giving.

I have two close friends whom I originally met years ago at funding appointments. Today we often get together without ever talking about the financial needs of my ministry. Why? Because they're my friends. We talk about our families, our interests, our lives. I seldom even ask them for anything anymore. In fact, they ask *me!* They're ready with a major gift before I'm ready to ask.

This is significant because it demonstrates the value of intimacy, and not just relational value to the donor. These men know that I know *when they like to give*. We are intimate enough that I am familiar with their work, their income situation, and their giving patterns. They also know that I know *what they like to give to*. Each person has unique God-given passions; each one feels led to support certain types of ministry projects or programs over other types. These men also know that I know *how much they can give*. We've been close enough for long enough that I am not likely to request a gift far under their capacity, or far over.

And finally, these friends know that if they give before I ask, they probably won't end up giving as much! Why? Because it's hard to turn your friends down. If I ask for a certain size of gift, they'll probably give it. If they offer a certain size of donation, I'll probably accept it. We're friends!

CHAPTER 5

After the Show

I served as executive pastor in each of two very large churches over the span of about 15 years. On any given Sunday, we would have as many as 300 visitors in our services. They typically visited because they saw or heard a service via television or radio, or they heard about the pastor's dynamic teaching. The worship was wonderful; the technical presentation was superb. People came to see what I privately called "the show."

But nobody *stayed* because of the show. They stayed if and only if they found *community* in the church. Did they form valuable relationships with other individuals in the church family? If so, they would continue to be a part of this ministry. If not, they would drive away — show or no.

On Monday morning the names of our church visitors landed on my desk, and my quest was to assimilate them into the life of the church. In sheer marketing terms, we had mounted a huge effort to get them in the door. But now came the more arduous, long-term challenge of weaving them into the fabric of the church. It needed to be done not simply for the sake of "growing the church," but for the sake of growing the people whom God had brought to us.

We developed a strategy of "high touch" — making a number of different types of personal contacts with the newcomer within the first three weeks after his or her initial visit, in hopes of making at least one lasting connection. Likewise in major donor ministry, we must devote ourselves not just to the goal of acquiring the gift, but to the relationship, the life of the donor, *after* the gift is given. A donor may give his first gift as the result of an appeal to his compassion, or because of the urgency of the appeal. But a donor will only *continue* to give as the result of the relationship he forms and the ministry he receives from the organization.

> *We must devote ourselves not just to the goal of acquiring the gift, but to the relationship, the life of the donor, after the gift is given.*

Many in major donor ministry insist that donor *acquisition* is hard and donor *retention* is easy. I beg to differ. Yes, it can be difficult and costly to acquire donors, but I find it far more challenging — and satisfying — to retain a donor over a long period of time. To stay in relationship, and to keep finding new ways to express the vision of the ministry within the context of that relationship, takes thought and prayer and time and effort.

In any donor relationship, I am constantly asking myself, Where do the interests of the organization intersect with the interests of the donor? Where can the great over-arching mission of the organization connect to the passions of the donor? Once in a while, certainly, you find a donor who has little or no interest in what your organization is doing. But more often, God has brought you together for a productive reason. There's at least an initial spark of interest in the donor for what your ministry is accomplishing. And the more he learns, the more interested he becomes.

Where do the interests of the organization intersect with the interests of the donor?

For years I have been associated with a great youth ministry located in the Midwest. It was always a wonderful experience to see a donor attend a Saturday night youth rally: 1,600 teens "rocking out" in worship to God — and then, the moment the speaker stepped onstage, *total silence.* At the end of the evening, hundreds of kids would be drawn to a closer walk with Christ. Tears would stream down the donor's face as they saw the fulfillment of their investment. The ministry rep may have asked that donor to pay for the sound system, or the projector, or some other piece of equipment. But they were really giving to see a teenager walk into the prayer room. In that moment, the donor would know for sure that he was investing well — giving according to his God-given passion.

The longer I maintain a friendship with a donor, the richer his experience with the ministry becomes. But at the same time, our friendship is growing richer. It eventually grows beyond the point of my ministering to him; in a well-developed friendship, we will minister to each other. In many cases, I find myself developing a level of intimacy with a donor that sometimes he doesn't even have with his pastor. This is no reflection on the pastor; it's simply a consequence of my consistent and intensely personal search for ways to be of value to that individual.

One of my best friends — I'll call him Alan — works in the financial management business. He gives away most of his income, much of it in passionate support of foreign missionaries. One day Alan informed me that he was going to shut down his ultra-lucrative agency and take his family to the mission field.

I sensed profoundly that he was making an emotional decision, that God was not actually calling him to the mission field personally. Over the weeks and months that followed, we spent many long hours discussing the decision. I felt strongly that his calling was clear: he was personally sending *ten new missionaries* into the field *every year*. He was making a phenomenal impact on world missions. His was a virtually irreplaceable ministry.

Months went by, we talked together and prayed together and pored over the Scriptures together — and finally one day, Alan nodded.

"You're right," he said. "I'm exactly where I'm supposed to be. My job is to send them."

I had borne the "joyful burden" of being his friend and helping him avoid an extremely dangerous mistake.

I had another good friend, a retired U.S. Marine I'll call Paul, who was the chief operating officer for a government agency. As I got to know him as a donor, I discovered that he too felt led to retire from his work and enter fulltime ministry. But in this case, I sensed that it was truly God's idea. He had always complained about inefficiencies in the operations of local churches. I urged Paul to "do something about it." He decided to go into ministry.

He needed to understand some of the harsh realities of ministry (he wouldn't be able to stomp his feet and get his way as he could from his perch as chief operating officer, for

30

example); I was able to coach him through the transition. Today Paul is serving on the staff of a church and ministering to ministries all over the country completely free of charge, as he lives off of his military and government pensions. What a privilege to walk with this man of God as he followed the leading of the Spirit! And this, again, was a relationship originally born of a *fundraising challenge*.

Another dear friend I'll call James. He was one of the students I mentored in the Northeast as a youth pastor in the 1970s. When I returned to this ministry as a consultant, years later, James and I hooked up again. By now he was a senior salesman for a big company, with a 16-state territory and $1 million in stock options alone. But he was giving only $200 a year in contributions to the ministry which had led him to faith in Christ!

As our friendship deepened, James expressed an interest in helping the ministry financially. He told me he would sell a piece of stock and contribute $3,000 to the latest project. I asked him if he realized that he could save on capital gains taxes if he just gave us the stock. He realized that he could give more; and he had decided to give $5,000.

James grew in his giving. Within two years he was giving $30,000; several years ago I challenged him to give $200,000 a year.

Then one day, he didn't return my call. I began to find that it was difficult to get hold of him by phone. Over the course of several months, I found I couldn't track him down. When I finally got with him, he seemed preoccupied. What's going on? I asked him. *Oh man, they keep putting new sales territories on me*, he replied.

But something seemed more deeply wrong.

One day James called me out of the blue. *Can you meet*

with me today? he wanted to know. I thought he was going to make a huge contribution to our current capital campaign.

Sitting across from me in a restaurant, James looked down at the table and said, "I've left my wife."

He had become involved with another woman several months earlier. He had gone to a counselor, but he had still walked away from his marriage. He had confessed to the leadership of his church; they had responded by dismissing him and demanding a public apology before he could return. He was crashing.

"There's no one else I have confidence in," he said to me.

> *I sometimes feel like more of a priest to donors than a field representative for a ministry.*

I was deeply humbled. We spent three hours mostly crying together. We talked about the implications for his teenage children. My heart grieved for him.

By the end of that conversation, with God's help, James had made the decision to head back home, to try to work it out. As I write these words, he is still at home, and still fighting fiercely against overwhelming odds. It was my privilege to be there for him, in the moment of crisis — no longer a fundraiser, just a friend.

I sometimes feel like more of a priest to donors than a field representative for a ministry; I am awed by the trust placed in me. And yet, through all the ups and downs of these relationships, God enables us to raise money for the mission of the organization. I challenged James to become the biggest donor in the history of this great ministry; he has set his sights on giving $1 million a year now. Yet I am also holding him accountable for his marriage, as a friend and mentor. This is clearly the product of a relationship I have built up over many years with him — by God's grace!

* * *

One day my wife informed me that she wanted another life. Without warning, she walked away from me and our three children. I was shattered. But my three friends — Alan, Paul, and James — supported me. As I tried to explain to my kids why their mother had left, one of these men was scheduling a plane to bring my sister and her husband to me because they could not afford to fly commercial. My relationship with him was not just about money. And it was not just about my investment in these friends. They were caring for me in crucial ways at a critical time in my life.

When someone pursues genuine ministry to major donors, he finds that he has opportunities to do much more than simply raise funds.

I admonish people in major donor ministry to get a handle on the powerful role they can play in the lives of others, and the wonderful enrichment they can experience by developing authentic relationships with donors. When someone pursues genuine *ministry* to major donors, he finds that he has opportunities to do much more than simply raise funds. This is not just about the stewarding of financial resources; it's the stewarding of a person. The relationship is more valuable than the record of giving; the donor is more valuable than the donations.

The relationship is more valuable than the record of giving; the donor is more valuable than the donations.

CHAPTER 6

What Are We About?

It seems almost infantile to say that major donor ministry has to begin with the organization's mission — indeed, it must *always* be linked to the organization's mission. But in fact, many ministry organizations have sent representatives into the field to cultivate major donors without first establishing a strong sense of what the organization is really about. The rep, then, goes into battle poorly armed. He can talk about the financial need of the ministry, he can complain about the faltering economy, he can discuss the "competition" and how they make it so difficult to raise money. But he can't articulate the mission of his organization — and that mission is at the heart of any authentically inspired contribution that a major donor might make.

The board of directors of a major ministry organization invited me to conduct a seminar for them. At the beginning of the session, I asked, "How many of you can state the mission of this ministry?" One board member seated across the table from me began to recite a very long statement of mission and purpose. But he was squinting strangely. Then I noticed the others; they were all squinting, and looking over my right

They looked at me as though I had asked them to quote the U.S. Constitution word for word.

shoulder. He was reading from a poster on the wall behind me. I laughed and stood up, blocking his view. "Now tell me your mission," I demanded. It was impossible. No member of that board could recite the mission statement of their own organization; it was simply too long and complicated to get a handle on.

A few days later I sat with four board members of a small ministry who were preparing to begin a major capital campaign. "Tell me your ministry's mission statement," I began. They looked at me as though I had asked them to quote the U.S. Constitution word for word. Even though the official mission statement was brief and manageable, it wasn't a bit important to the leaders of the organization.

In both of these cases — as in hundreds of ministry organizations — there's a failure to grasp the vital importance of the "mission." What is our organization about? Everyone involved in the ministry, from the chairman of the board to the maintenance staff, ought to understand what the organization is there to do. The

The donor, likewise, needs to be told, and "sold," on the specific mission of the ministry.

donor, likewise, needs to be told, and "sold," on the specific mission of the ministry.

The mission statement can't be a long-winded description

of everything the organization does. And it can't be a meaningless slogan or cliché. It has to be a simple, straightforward statement of why the organization exists.

I'm proud of ministries that take this seriously and invest in the achievement of this goal.

Some years ago the leadership team of one ministry actually retreated to the cornfields of Iowa to spend several days and nights nailing down the organization's mission statement. As they debated what they were really about, the long and difficult discussions revealed discrepancies between the perspectives of various leaders in the organization.

The mission of your organization should be the foundation of every conversation you have with a major donor about your ministry.

Even more importantly, those days of intensive thought, prayer, and debate — with the goal of reducing the mission to a single, over-arching statement — led to the emergence of a new *global* emphasis for this organization. Their talks helped them crystallize the leading of the Lord, which each of them had felt but which none of them had brought to the table. Arm-wrestling over the organization's mission statement actually helped to crystallize a new worldwide vision — which literally reinvented the organization in the ensuing years.

The mission of your organization should be the foundation of every conversation you have with a major donor about your ministry. You may discuss a hundred different aspects of the ministry, of the current campaign, of this or that — but underneath it all is the *mission*. The mission of your organization is the reason you are involved in it, giving your life to it. Your passion for that mission — the God-given calling of your organization — is what will spark the interest of that donor, if the donor's interest is ever to be sparked at all.

* * *

While the organization's mission statement must be kept in sharp focus by every staff member, top to bottom, this laser-sharp focus is of particularly vital importance to the individual ministry representative. Why? Because it's so easy to get wrapped up in a relationship and forget to raise money *for the organization's mission!*

Here's how a serious problem can develop — depending on the internal wiring of the individual field representative.

Those who love the idea of ministering to people personally, developing strong friendships and enduring relationships, tend to gravitate to this model of major donor ministry because it involves no pressure tactics or arm-twisting. But this same type of person also sometimes tends to let the financial goals drift. These reps get lost in the relationship. But ultimately, as a matter of integrity and the stewardship of the ministry's resources, a rep must keep the mission of the organization in focus. That mission can't be accomplished if the ministry's representatives form friendships without collecting donations.

That mission can't be accomplished if the ministry's representatives form friendships without collecting donations.

I have sometimes been forced to release some ministry representatives because they could not manage both the warm relationship and the "closing of the sale." I hired Deborah with high hopes; she had tremendous credentials as a salesperson in the radio industry. At 27, fresh out of school, she wowed absolutely everyone who met her. She was eager to move into ministry. I hired her the day I met her. Four months later, she hadn't raised a dollar. "I'm just building those relationships," she explained. At eight months, she still hadn't raised any money. By now I'm beginning to lean on her a little. But she was struggling. She loved the people she was working with; she simply couldn't ask them for money. For a few weeks I accompanied her on calls to donors. It was clear that the donors adored her. She had clearly laid the groundwork for a donation to be requested and received. I tried to demonstrate how easy the final step could be.

"John, Alice, I know you've developed a great friendship with Deborah," I would say. "Do you have any questions about the ministry that she and I are working with?" No, they didn't. "Great. Is there any reason based on what you know about us and what you've seen that you wouldn't want to participate with us as a donor?" No, not at all. "Well, great. Here's a chart of our giving levels for the campaign we're working on right now. Where do you see yourself fitting in?" Well, we could give a thousand dollars. "Wonderful! How would you like us to follow up with you on that?..." And so forth. Day after day, I asked Deborah's donors for money. Day after day, they gave major gifts.

After two months of demonstrations like this, I assured Deborah that she could do it too. "It's not hard," I assured her. "You've got the relationships. They're not giving because of me; they're giving because of you." Two more months went by. Deborah had still not raised one dollar. For the sake of the ministry, I had to let her go. She wept bitterly. "I don't know what's wrong with me. I sold radio time. There's something about this. It's just hard for me to ask."

Howard was in his mid-40s. He was a super sales guy. We

offered him a nice salary. He was convinced he could raise a lot of money fast. But he raised only a small amount of money in the first six months. He complained that he was being given poor prospects, but I went on calls with him and observed that he was getting lost in the relationships. He was forgetting the mission of the ministry, and his own mission; he was forgetting why he was there. There is a time to concentrate on the relationship, and there is a time in a relationship when it's appropriate to ask for money. Howard was unable to "pull the trigger" and ask his new friends for money. He was also unwilling to say, "I can't do this." I had to fire him.

Patricia was among the best sales representatives that one office equipment company had ever had in the Southwest. She was gorgeous; she sold $80,000 in office equipment every month. We hired her enthusiastically. But she could not ask people for money. What's the problem? I asked her. She wept profusely. "I just can't ask them," she said. "I'm afraid they'll tell me no!" I worked with her a long time, but to no avail.

The first person I ever trained in major donor ministry was a woman named Chris Cole. At 26, she had no fundraising background, but she had a passion for the ministry. I trained her, went on calls with her — and within six months, she was raising 40% more than her wage.

Because she was our first field rep, we had no significant pool of donors. She had no choice but to make a lot of "cold calls," contacting prospects out of the blue and asking for the opportunity to get together and talk about the ministry. I warned her that she would get a lot of no's before she would ever get a yes — statistically, it was likely that she would be rejected eight times for every *one* acceptance. Half an hour into her first day at work, as I sat at my desk, I heard her calling down the hall: "I'm halfway to a yes!" She had been turned down four times. But she was persistent. She was engaging. When she got into a relationship with someone, she never forgot the mission: the mission of the organization she was representing, which filled her with joy and energy, and her specific mission as a field representative of that organization: to raise money for the achievement of the organization's ministry goals.

When she got into a relationship with someone, she never forgot the mission.

One of the most generous donors I've ever worked with — I'll call him Terry — contributes generously to a ministry I have worked with in the past. He serves on its board. After an incident in which a student was injured at one of the ministry's summer camps, Terry called me posing as a belligerent southerner who had heard about the trouble. He railed about the dangers of sending children to our camps. I recognized his voice but pretended not to. Instead, I explained that I could have a member of the board call on him about his concerns. However, I intimated, the board members were "really not all that committed"; they more or less served in hopes of getting "free stuff" from the organization. After we had both cracked up, I told Terry that we were working on a new scholarship project, and I wanted to get with him to talk about it. In spite of our fun, crazy interaction, the mission is always at the forefront of the relationship. I make sure it stays there, and Terry never loses sight of the fact that the mission of the ministry is hugely important — so I'm going to be bringing it up again. Yes, the relationship is real, but I am also systematic about the mission.

41

It is important that a field representative feel a sense of "the calling of God" into major donor ministry. If a rep feels led by God into this work, the mission of the organization will tend to stay in sharper focus for him. If a ministry's representative, for example, believes that God has called him there "to help students grow into a growing relationship with Jesus Christ" (that organization's mission statement), he will do everything — build relationships, work hard, etc. — with a strong level of commitment and a rather slim chance of being sidetracked.

If a rep feels led by God into this work, the mission of the organization will tend to stay in sharper focus for him.

When I am face to face with a donor, I have to be able to trust my mission. I have to know it, understand it, and believe it. I have to be committed to it heart and soul. My heart has to beat with the pulse of that mission. Then, every interaction with that donor, every conversation — all the way from chit-chat about casual everyday goings-on to the "moment of truth" when I'm asking for a donation — will flow naturally out of, and back to, that mission. If the rep isn't sold on it, the donor is unlikely to buy into it.

Stewardship requires vigilance. "Stewardship drift" is natural.

* * *

Stewardship requires vigilance. "Stewardship drift" is natural. On my first day as executive pastor at a large church in Arizona, I was shocked to discover that the organization had no budget. They were bringing in close to $5 million a year, but there was no system for allocating funds — and no way to gauge the effectiveness of spending decisions. I immediately called together the heads of the various ministry departments.

"It may not be much," I told them, "but we're going to have a budget when we go home today — because I'm not coming back to work tomorrow without one!" I couldn't honestly report to the board on the church's activities, or reasonably plan for the future, if I didn't have a spending plan.

Out of that first primitive number-crunching session, I discovered that the church was spending a breathtaking amount of money in salaries. I nosed around to find out why. Soon it became clear. The unconscious but prevailing attitude was *Why ask for a volunteer when we can hire someone?* The church had come to trust in its income — and was unintentionally squandering hundreds of thousands of dollars in the process. They were also cheating dozens of church members out of the blessings that come through service.

We began to shift the philosophy of the church. We began to shift paid positions to volunteer status (in effect diversifying our sources of labor). I was sometimes called the "hatchet man." But we brought our payroll down from $1.5 million to less than $1 million without any reduction in ministry. We could honestly say that every penny given to the church was achieving as much ministry as possible.

Someone assigned to work with major donors must not only truly minister to them, but also truly raise money from them!

We have to give aggressive, ongoing attention to the stewardship of our ministry's resources in the major donor area. Someone assigned to work with major donors must not only truly minister to them, but also truly raise money from them!

43

CHAPTER 7

Culture Shock

There was once a ministry organization that went through development directors at a rate of about one a year. The fifth development director in the queue was fearful for his job, but nonetheless determined to figure out what strange poison in the organization kept killing off development directors.

As he explored, he found that the organization was more than 50 years old but had never cultivated personal relationships with any of its donors. As a result, they were raising virtually all of their revenue in $10 and $25 contributions through direct mail — and had fewer than 15 contributors who would qualify as major donors.

He also discovered a huge, invisible chasm between the staff members who "did ministry" and the staff members who "did development." Like a corporation with a problematic disconnect between sales and service, this ministry had no integration, no overlap, no interrelationships between "ministry"

He also discovered a huge, invisible chasm between the staff members who "did ministry" and the staff members who "did development."

and "marketing."

So the development director began an effort to change the thinking of the entire staff — to persuade "marketing people" that they were actually in ministry, and persuade "ministry people" that they were vital to the marketing success of the organization.

First, he began training the development staff in the importance of being highly engaged in ministry. For the first time ever, ministry representatives began attending ministry functions, got involved in the actual work of the ministry, both locally and out of town. (Typical response of a ministry staffer on seeing a development staffer at a ministry event: "What are *you* doing here?")

Then the development director began guiding the "ministry team" through development training. They learned to think in terms of their own broad scope of personal contacts and influence. A ministry staff member, after all, comes in contact with hundreds of people over the course of a year who might become involved with the ministry — if that staff member were only tuned in to their potential.

Before long, staff members in that organization began to cultivate major donor relationships. Their training had showed them how to maintain and

A ministry staff member, after all, comes in contact with hundreds of people over the course of a year who might become involved with the ministry — if that staff member were only tuned in to their potential.

track those relationships in relatively simple ways. Soon, three or four of the ministry staff members were bringing major gifts into the organization through their personal relationships. To this day, although their "job description" is still "exclusively" about "ministry," they are truly involved in major donor ministry!

The entire organization needs to understand and embrace and commit to the relational development philosophy of the ministry. It cannot simply be something the "marketing guys do." But to achieve such a radical infusion of development philosophy into a staff means taking a hard look at every process and every system in the organization. What does this worker do? How do we measure his success? What does this worker believe he *should* be doing? What would a relational philosophy of ministry require this worker to do differently? How *should* we be measuring this worker's success? Will this worker embrace the new idea? These can be painful questions, and the answers can be more painful still. But they are crucial to the achievement of a new "culture." And it's an entire culture that is needed — an alignment of everybody, every function, to the priority of establishing and maintaining authentic relationships with donors.

Many ministries contact our agency for help with major donors, only to be disappointed when we insist that an entire ministry culture must be established in order for the organization to achieve maximum success. They want a "program" that they can "add" to what they are doing; they want to be able to "contract for" (that is, *buy*) major donors

The entire organization needs to understand and embrace and commit to the relational development philosophy of the ministry.

and major donations. But such an approach will produce less satisfying and shorter-term results. Cultivating quality friendships with major donors will produce more satisfying, longer-term results. You can build the future of your ministry on quality relationships with major donors.

Cultivating quality friendships with major donors will produce more satisfying, longer-term results. You can build the future of your ministry on quality relationships with major donors.

Some organizations want to "go relational" in parts of their operation, but don't want to bother involving certain portions of their staff or adjusting certain systems. In many cases, the reasons are political. "Barbara" has such a high sense of ownership of her functions that nobody wants to challenge her. Or "Dick" is so difficult to work with that everybody assures everybody else that he can never change — in order to avoid the confrontation. But to allow philosophical inconsistencies within an organization is always deadly. Do the hard work of integrating your entire organization into a new way of thinking — create a true culture — and you'll take your ministry to a whole new level.

The staff came to understand that everyone does development.

The fifth development director managed to survive. He took his hits, but he hung on. One day it was as if a light bulb went on, and the staff came to understand that *everyone does development.* "We were driven by our mission, yes," the development director says. "But the culture of our organization was finally becoming integrated with an understanding that we all needed to embrace financial development as a worthy cause, if we were to ultimately succeed."

* * *

Some years ago I was hired to serve as development director by a ministry organization. I suggested because of the organization's history that it might be wise for the management team not to announce my arrival with a lot of fanfare. I wanted to be able to assess the staff's attitudes about their donors and about fundraising without a lot of barriers.

Based on the ministry's needs of the moment, the management team and I developed a relatively small project — with a goal of just $60,000 — which would meet a real need in the ministry but would also give me a good reason to call the largest donors and introduce myself. To get started, I walked into the ministry's donor records office to get a breakdown of the organization's top 500 donors. The woman at the desk looked at me suspiciously.

"And who are you?" she asked coldly.

"I'm Tim Smith," I replied with a smile. "I work in development here, and I need a list of our top donors, so I can start working out a plan for calling them."

"I'm sorry, but you're not authorized to see that list," the woman replied.

I was dumbfounded. I don't remember what I said. I walked back to my office, stunned.

Within five minutes, the chief operating officer of the ministry was in my office, apologizing. "She's just a little protective of the donor base," he explained. "It's like her baby."

This experience typified the culture of the organization. The "ministry guys" were in one corner. The "development guys" were in the basement. "Administration" was in a third sector, and their job was "campus cop": *We gotta keep an eye on these ministry guys, to make sure they're working hard and doing things the way we want them done. And we gotta keep an eye on these development guys, or they'll just spend us blind, trying to raise money.* This wasn't spoken; it was unspoken, and just as poisonous.

I came away from that initial exploration with two strong convictions: first, the donors had been allowed to fall totally out of touch with the organization; and second, there was no sense of partnership in the culture of the organization, either between various staff members or between donors and staff.

When I finally got my list of donors, I began calling them. The response was jarring. "What do you want?" one demanded. "Why are you calling me?" another asked. "Nobody ever called me before!" one groused. "What's going on with you guys?" They were hostile. Clearly, no personal relationship had ever been cultivated.

But I persisted; I eventually got a few appointments to see donors face-to-face. In those situations, I made it a point to ask how the donor felt about the ministry organization. They would routinely turn wistful and speak fondly about events and programs that had occurred *decades earlier.* They talked about them in the present tense — clearly unaware that the ministry had done anything new or different in the past 15 or 20 years!

I came away from that initial exploration with two strong convictions: first, the donors had been allowed to fall totally out of touch with the organization; and second, there was no sense of partnership in the culture of the organization, either between various staff members or between donors and staff. There was no sense of "we're doing this together."

I took the ministry's top two executives to lunch and gave them my assessments: Our ministry team saw our development team as an appendage to the organization, a necessary evil — *Keep them out of sight, out of mind, as much as possible* seemed to be the prevailing attitude. Our development team felt that nobody liked them, nobody understood them, nobody talked to them — and they were right. One ministry staffer had informed me of his belief that the entire staff should sign off on every fundraising letter before it went out, to make sure that nobody disagreed with any of the wording. Such a policy would have crippled the system — but the staffer who suggested it was dead serious. The development team was a threat, as far as he was concerned, to the integrity of the ministry. One staffer who, like many in ministry organizations, raised his own support, admonished me never to send an appeal for the organization at large to individuals who supported him personally. His own part in the ministry had become his exclusive priority; the organization had become the enemy.

"This is a very dysfunctional environment," I told the executives. The only advice I could give was to tear it down. We needed to begin a systematic program of educating and inspiring the entire staff with regard to how we all fit together — in ministry, in administration, and in fundraising — and how one arm could not be considered more significant than any other. I warned the executives of the ramifications of such a decision. We would likely be forced to let a number of people go, because they would be unable to make the transition. It would take quite a long time, too; I estimated a year.

The executives courageously agreed. By God's grace, only one member of the development team resigned. In donor records, the guardian angel of data entry departed; I replaced her with a keen-eyed, ministry-passionate worker who would zero in on any fluctuation in a donor's giving pattern and alert me, so I could follow up with the donor. (One donor suddenly jumped from $2,000 a year to $26,000 a year; the data entry person, trained to think "How can I serve the team?" rather than "This is my baby," was the first to call my attention to the change.) We hired a systems director to build a means of tracking donor activity. We hired field representatives and trained them in caring for donors authentically. Most challenging of all, we gathered the entire staff for a series of six major "acculturation" sessions. In these, we taught the staff to see themselves as vitally important to all three aspects of the organization's operation: administration, development, and the ministry "program" itself.

For the first time ever, development personnel started attending ministry events, showing an interest in the "product" they were marketing, asking questions and gaining an understanding of the ministry process.

For the first time ever, development personnel started attending ministry events, showing an interest in the "product" they were marketing, asking questions and gaining an understanding of the ministry process. Initial suspicion on the part of ministry staff eventually gave way to appreciation for the support. Development workers gradually offered to assume some of the ministry functions; with their instincts they were able to adjust those activities, creating opportunities for connections with prospective donors where none had existed before — without diminishing the ministry value of the events. Those connections were soon producing enormous amounts of revenue for the ministry, through follow-ups by our field representatives. Eventually, newly hired field reps were required to experience the full range of the ministry's activities before calling on donors.

> *The staff members formerly isolated in "doing ministry" came to see their potential as the "eyes and ears" of the development operation.*

Along the way, the staff members formerly isolated in "doing ministry" came to see their potential as the "eyes and ears" of the development operation. At one point we began sending our ministry staff through the same training that field reps received, to give them a full understanding of how to talk effectively with donors and prospects about the ministry.

Finally, we shifted the thinking of administrative personnel. They came to realize that they were there to support, not to control. They could be virtually invisible and still fulfill their God-given role brilliantly.

That organization became a healthy culture of mutual trust and respect. Misunderstandings evaporated. We no longer heard complaints like "Those development guys don't do anything but go to lunch" and "Those ministry guys have no idea how hard I'm working to provide their paycheck." Every member of the team was supportive of the role of every other member.

* * *

There's an extra advantage to cross-training staff members so that ministry workers can deal well with donors: in some cases, the best relational "fit" with a major donor may not be a field rep, but a ministry staffer. My friend Eric was a dynamic Christian youth worker; he made a tremendous impact on the children of a wealthy family in our community. Our ministry wanted to give this family an opportunity to consider financially supporting various projects, but we had no entré. Eric served on our ministry staff, but certainly not in fundraising — yet he had the ability to pick up the phone and make a date with the head of that family. Because Eric had been trained in major donor ministry, and because he embraced the idea that giving to our ministry was a good thing, he was able to make that contact. "Hey, how's it going?" the conversation began. From there it led to "Hey, can I come by and talk to you about a new project that our ministry is doing, and see if you'd like to be involved?" It was natural, it was casual — and it was hugely valuable to the ministry! No field rep could have done it as easily or as well, if at all.

In some cases, the best relational "fit" with a major donor may not be a field rep, but a ministry staffer.

This was not a question of who was the most persuasive fundraiser in the organization; it was a question of who is the best person for the relationship? But you can't convince a minister to represent the financial needs of the organization to a donor if he hasn't been trained and inspired to see himself as part of a culture that is thoroughly arranged around and committed to the mission of the organization. Eric saw the ministry dynamic of fundraising, and rose to the challenge. He understood that it would be more than good for the organization if that family became donors; it would be good for that family as well.

* * *

Trained, inspired staff members see and seize opportunities to connect with donors. A ministry to inner-city youth was preparing to restrict its summer camps to kids from certain areas because their facilities were simply too jammed to hold all the kids. A guy walked into the camp and asked one of the workers about the rumor; the kids from his own community would be excluded. Yes, the worker replied, the cutback would happen. "What would it take to change things?" the visitor asked. "A new building? My church has an endowment. Maybe we could build a new building, big enough for 80 kids. That's how many kids we normally bring."

> *Trained, inspired staff members see and seize opportunities to connect with donors.*

The worker scrambled for a phone and called me. He replayed the conversation for me, then asked, "Can you get down here and talk to this guy?"

"You talk to him!" I replied. "You're there. It will take me an hour to get there."

"Well, get here as fast as you can," he insisted.

When I arrived at the campground, the worker had already nailed down the commitment. His training had kicked in. If I had trained him better, he might not have needed to call me at all! But in reality, if he had found himself in the same situation just one year earlier, he might have completely missed the opportunity. Perhaps he would have mumbled, "I could give you Tim Smith's phone number," but that would have been the extent of the connection. This was a staffer who, during my training of the staff, had resisted the notion of getting involved in fundraising. ("Development guys should do their job, we ministry guys should do our job," he had said.)

Someday there might be a new 80-bed building at that campground because that ministry organization had developed among its staff a culture of enthusiasm for engaging donors.

An old airline commercial has a CEO walking into a room full of the company's salespeople and reporting the loss of the firm's oldest and largest client. Why did they split? Because we were out of touch, he says. The CEO hands an airline ticket to each salesperson. What are these for? We're going to visit our friends — our customers. Then we see that the CEO has a plane ticket in his own pocket. Where are you going? I'm going to see our oldest friend, he says, the one who just fired us.

> *It doesn't matter how old and established my ministry organization may be, if the donor feels I'm out of touch, his interests will gravitate elsewhere.*

This commercial reminds me that it doesn't matter how old and established my ministry organization may be, if the donor feels I'm out of touch, his interests will gravitate elsewhere. I can't afford to have a frontline ministry staffer encounter a donor or prospect and fail to connect or seize the moment. For the sake of the ministry, every staff member needs to be trained, motivated, inspired to reach out and make the most of every "divine encounter"! Indeed, the best person to talk about the ministry is the most passionate person — and the most passionate person is the person doing the ministry day in and day out. So it's wise to equip that ministry worker to talk effectively with any donor or prospect. This is not just about random encounters, either: every individual has certain people with whom he exercises influence. If a ministry staff member is trained to articulate the vision of his ministry, those with whom he has influence can discover more readily their level of interest in the work of the organization.

* * *

I once found myself assigned to a ministry situation where I "inherited" relationships with two fundraisers of many years' experience. I'll call them Hallowell and McFadden. Both were numbers-driven. McFadden had been a big-city sales-man with a massive corporation; he was always "working the numbers." Hallowell was the ultimate analytical thinker. Both men were sellers: 8 no's to every yes; 3 prospects for every gift you need; work the numbers. Everything was a formula. Acquiring a contribution was like a sale.

After a while I challenged both guys. "You're trying to turn me into a sales manager," I said. "If I wanted to be a sales manager, I could go some-where else and make a lot more money. This has to be about 'calling' and ministry."

If a ministry staff member is trained to articulate the vision of his ministry, those with whom he has influence can discover more readily their level of interest in the work of the organization.

McFadden erupted. His experience, he reminded me, spanned many more years — even decades — than mine. But he was consumed with results, figures, charts. All of that would be fine, I insisted, if it were integrated into a ministry mindset. But what we really needed were ministry representatives who were passionate about the mission of the organization, who would minister to donors through thriving personal friendships, and cast the vision authentically to those friends along the way.

Hallowell, on the other hand, was intrigued by the idea of a relational model for major donor ministry. He asked questions; we spent hours in productive discussion. He began doing things differently. To this day, he is ministering to major donors effectively. But McFadden moved on.

In order to create a culture conducive to relational major donor ministry, we have to get "over the hump" of thinking about this as a new kind of formula for success. It's about loving the people who support the ministry, believing that God's design makes people happier and healthier when they're giving, and inspiring them to step up to the fullness of their God-given role as supporters of his work.

People who focus exclusively on major donor ministry are just as surely ministers as people who spoon soup for the homeless or who teach the Bible from a pulpit.

People who "do ministry" do not need to see a move toward relationship with donors as a departure from their calling. It is an extension, a new facet, of their calling. People who focus exclusively on major donor ministry are just as surely ministers as people who spoon soup for the homeless or who teach the Bible from a pulpit. Donors need ministry just as surely as Sunday school attendees or recovering alcoholics. Those donors need the care and attention of a friend more than our ministry organization needs their money. But as they receive ministry from a person who is passionate about a certain organization, it is appropriate that their giving will flow toward the mission of that organization.

CHAPTER 8

Shifting Gears

How can you shift the culture of your ministry organization and inspire everyone to embrace development — so that every staff member, in effect, becomes a "field rep" for the ministry? Here are some steps to take:

1. Do a self-critique.

What do you believe about relationship-based, ministry-based fundraising?

What concerns you the most about how your ministry raises money?

One of our clients had a very large file of high-frequency donors. Whenever there was a crisis, their donors responded immediately. But they really had not developed relationships with these donors.

What concerns you the most about how your ministry raises money?

The leaders of the organization sensed that things needed

to be different. There were relatively few major donors to the ministry, and there was the feeling that these major donors were not being well treated. So the leadership of the ministry invited our agency to help them establish a valid major donor ministry.

We came in and trained their leadership team for several days in the philosophy and foundations of major donor relationships. The team was excited. They identified several ministry representatives to go out and begin to implement a relationship-based major donor effort.

But before things could even get off the ground, several staff members outside the fundraising department began to criticize the new efforts. These were well-intentioned people who had not been integrated into the development philosophy. The organization had asked us to train their leadership team, but *stopped short of creating a whole new culture in their organization.*

The negative comments of a few staff members began to undermine the efforts of the new ministry representatives assigned to major donors. We had to stop, back up, put out some fires, train some additional people, and try again. Several months were lost, and key opportunities were wasted, as a result of initiating a "program" instead of creating a "culture."

It's crucial to do a comprehensive self-critique, assessing the attitudes and concerns of the entire staff. This is especially true in smaller ministries where the voice of one disgruntled staff person can undermine the entire fundraising effort.

Take a close look at yourself and examine your workers' attitudes about fundraising and about building friendships with major donors. You may be surprised to discover that the staff of your ministry, like those of many ministries, thinks of fundraising as a necessary evil, something we "have no choice but to do." They may see fundraising as something the president of the organization should do. They may feel that major donors ought not to be singled out for any special attention.

> *You may be surprised to discover that the staff of your ministry, like those of many ministries, thinks of fundraising as a necessary evil, something we "have no choice but to do."*

Until we face our workers' own concerns and attitudes about fundraising, we cannot develop a new culture. Sometimes we have to rock our paradigms, or violate our comfort zones, in order to effect real change.

We were invited to work with a 40-year-old ministry organization which had perfected the art of acquiring and inspiring major donors through high-profile community events. But their organization was in disarray, and they were not reaching out effectively to smaller donors. We laid out a vision for reorganization, which was accepted, and we went to work. We worked with the president to create a letter which would ask donors for financial support. The letter went out — and one board member complained about its "tone." The president's response was to categorically ban appeal letters.

On my next visit to the ministry, I walked into a chaos of backbiting and finger-pointing. "They're not really

> *Sometimes we have to rock our paradigms, or violate our comfort zones, in order to effect real change.*

raising any money for us," the financial officer asserted. I asked to see the records for myself — and then showed the management team that in reality, our single appeal had generated

28% more income for the ministry than in the same time period a year before. The president relented; we continued mailing appeals. But month after month, factions of the staff resisted our every effort. The new systems created more work; the organization for the first time was actually asking for money in print — there were several new twists to be unhappy about. ("That won't work," the development director said, "I wouldn't respond to that." Do you feel you represent the donor base? I inquired. "I'm *here* to represent the donor base!" he snorted.)

Eventually the same disgruntled board member complained about a mailing, and the president responded by sending an apology to every donor on the file. I arrived for my next scheduled visit to the organization. The conflict was palpable. The president claimed that the most recent offending letter — although it bore his signature — had gone out without his ever seeing it, and did not "sound like" him. Then the communications director produced documentation proving that the president had indeed signed off on the letter, and was routinely signing off on everything that went into the mail. Or, perhaps, someone in the president's office was signing off for him? The president, as it turned out, was operating in his own world — too busy, in his own view, even to read the documents being given to him for his signature, but more than ready to blame those who had proceeded with his implied consent.

This kind of dysfunction existed throughout the organization: they were high on blaming and low on taking responsibility.

This kind of dysfunction existed throughout the organization: they were high on blaming and low on taking responsibility.

These tendencies militated against the creation of a team spirit or unified culture in the organization, and also made it extremely difficult for the organization to get the most out of any consultant's input. From the beginning of our professional relationship, we found this to be so. After they hired us but before we began our work, the president — operating in his own private universe — decided without warning to launch a massive $60 million capital campaign. The cause was enormously worthwhile, but the organization had never raised more than $5 million in a year. By the time we arrived, they had already fallen a million dollars short of their first-phase $3 million goal! They had not asked a single major donor in advance about their enthusiasm for such a project.

I suggested that it would have been better to talk face-to-face with all the top donors, and survey another 600, before committing to the project. (The study of feasibility is always the most important first step in a capital campaign. Here again, however, it requires clear-eyed self-inspection.) In any case, I recommended that we go talk to major donors who had declined to give to Phase I. The first two donors contacted literally had the capacity to fund the entire project themselves. But each of them, independent of the other, gave the same feedback: they believed the organization had drifted from its original mission. As the ministry had grown, the visionary leader had expanded its focus. But these major donors hadn't been kept in the loop; the organization hadn't stayed in close communication with them, so they hadn't grasped and become excited about the morphing vision. In order to survive, the organization eventually was forced to sell a portion of the property that it had hoped to build on through the capital campaign.

We continued to work with the ministry's leaders and staff.

They had enormous potential because of their tremendous major donor base. But they were unwilling to look at themselves critically, and they were certainly unable to accept an outsider's critical assessment. Every suggestion of a new approach was met with arch resistance. (Among our many roles, we were hired to improve the organization's newsletter. But the staff member in charge of the newsletter refused every change we suggested. "That's just not *us*," he insisted. "The president doesn't like it." I would have to place a call to the president's office and get his explicit approval. Then I would call the newsletter manager back. "Okay, it's your neck," he would reply.) Ultimately, they could not change their culture. In fact, they continually reinforced their dysfunction. Finally, we had no choice but to part company.

> *A successful ministry will look at itself and ask, What's wrong with our environment? Are there values in this culture that keep our staff from integrating into a single team?*

A successful ministry will look at itself and ask, What's wrong with our environment? Are there values in this culture that keep our staff from integrating into a single team?

2. Become a student.

When a ministry asks our agency to help them with major donors, I always push the leaders to read. I want ministry personnel to be exposed to new ways of thinking about fundraising, well beyond the input that we can offer. There are innumerable resources available that will help to focus one's thinking on the relational element of fundraising.

Books that challenged me to re-think my traditional understanding of fundraising include:

Generous Living by Ron Blue. This book explains volumes about the "mind" of the donor. What motivates and challenges a donor to give? And when does a donor feel fulfilled?

The Prospering Para-church by Wesley K. Wilmer & J. David Schmidt with Martyn Smith. This is the book that first inspired me to think of donors as stakeholders in the ministry.

Seven Deadly Diseases of Ministry Marketing by Doug Brendel with E. Dale Berkey and Jack W. Sheline. This book, produced by our agency, has really re-vamped many ministries' approach to the subject of marketing. The core of this book takes you into the heart of service and ministry to the donor.

Good to Great by Jim Collins. How to take a good organization up a step.

The Treasure Principle by Randy Alcorn. A great little inspirational book that says generosity is part of God's design and ought to be encouraged. He talks about the dot and the line. Many ministries focus on the dot — how a gift will impact the ministry today. But the emphasis ought to be on the line — how a gift will impact *you* as the donor, and others over the course of eternity.

God Owns My Stuff by Wes Wilmer.

3. Study successful ministries.

Many successful ministries have figured out major donor relationships. Our agency has studied those ministries and talked to their leaders. In every case, without fail, they led us back to the central concept of serving the donor as a friend, in an authentic personal relationship. Major donors are not simply cogs in the machinery of a fundraising program; they are not statistics on a revenue graph. They are people. But we also observe that the most successful ministries have not simply targeted donors from a single department of their organization; they have created an entire culture in which every staff member, regardless of his function, sees *giving to the ministry* as valid and valuable.

> *Major donors are not simply cogs in the machinery of a fundraising program; they are not statistics on a revenue graph. They are people.*

In our work as an agency "ministering to ministries," one of the most important roles we can play is in the honest evaluation of where a troubled ministry "went off track." We most often observe that the potential for an integrated "culture" has been disrupted by one or more of the "deadly diseases of ministry marketing" that we discussed in that book. Springboarding off of those well-established truths, we can say with authority that you'll be frustrated in your attempts to create a new culture:

- If some or all of your personnel can't articulate the mission of the organization in a single sentence from memory.

   One ministry leader gave each ministry staff member a card with the organization's new mission statement printed on it. He challenged everyone in the organization to memorize it, internalize it, and think up some way to talk about it from the "first person" perspective. Some time later he toured the facilities. "Tell me the mission statement," he would say, "and what it means to you." Staffers who succeeded got to choose between a handful of Barnes & Noble gift certificates and a handful of vouchers for free tickets to the movies!

- If your staff has the mission nailed down but isn't willing to talk enthusiastically about the ministry outside the workplace.

•If your fundraising department is isolated from the departments "doing the ministry."

A high-profile ministry in the western United States was struggling. We talked to their donors and discovered utter confusion about the organization's ministry activities. The ministry appeared to be doing its mission — while the marketing department was promoting the purchase of products which the donors perceived as unrelated to the organization's mission. (No problem offering products, but the marketing staff must present these products in the context of the mission in order for the donors to "get it.")

•If you are unwilling to invest actual money into a fundraising effort, into a relationship-building effort, and into a donor-thanking effort.

Chosen People Ministries has been impressive in this regard. As I write these words, their major donor representative is on a world tour with only one goal: to thank every major donor face-to-face for his support of the ministry. Montrose Bible Conference, too, has relentlessly invested in the nurturing of relationships with donors.

Many ministries have found that *thanked donors* and *speedily thanked donors* give more generously than *unthanked donors* or *belatedly thanked* donors. A personalized thank-you note promptly mailed with a receipt for a donation can generate another gift from the donor who has just given! Some organizations have found that as much as 65% of their revenue can flow from such a "receipt package"!

One of our clients who works in ministry to high school students began a program of selecting students who had been touched by the ministry, bringing them into their ministry offices, stoking them with pizza and Cokes, and having them call donors simply to say "thank you" for their support of the organization. The chemistry between teens and donors was incredible. One very average-looking teenager, I'll call him Mickey, was too effervescent to stay on any kind of "script." He would thank the donor, but then the conversation would *evolve*. By the time he hung up, he had made a new friend. A few days later they received a letter from a donor thanking *them* for Mickey's call — with a $2,500 check enclosed.

> *A personalized thank-you note promptly mailed with a receipt for a donation can generate another gift from the donor who has just given!*

Healthy ministries will invest in the expression of appreciation to donors. And those words of affirmation will deepen the donors' commitment to the mission of the organization!

• If you don't see and understand the biblical validity of good ministry marketing.

• If you don't have a healthy management system which allows for adequate advance planning of strategies, including crucial team-to-team communication within the organization.

• If your communications with donors are based on erroneous assumptions about them (the donors think "just like we do," or are essentially inferior) — rather than the view that donors are people too, and should be seen for who they are, and communicated with accordingly.

Numerous ministries struggle in particular with the view that "the donors think just like we do." They are clueless about the real mentality of their donors and the impact of their communications on their donors.

A ministry rep who served in major donor ministry tells this rather unnerving story:

En route to a social event, it so happened that a ministry leader and his wife ended up in the same vehicle as an extremely wealthy couple who were friends of the ministry rep. At the event, the ministry leader took the rep aside and raved about the wealthy couple's wonderful fascination with the ministry.

The rep's stomach tightened. A little while later, as he feared, his wealthy friends took him aside. They were still disgusted by their encounter with the ministry leader. They had tried to be polite, but the ministry leader and his wife were cluelessly boring and self-absorbed, talking endlessly about themselves and their mission. The ministry rep had to do damage control with the potential donors because of the ministry leader's insensitivity.

Numerous ministries struggle in particular with the view that "the donors think just like we do."

Successful ministries genuinely tune in to their donors; they don't fixate on themselves. (This is especially difficult for personality-based ministries.) Donors need enough information to make a decision about giving; they don't need to know everything the ministry leader thinks and feels and believes and wants! Many ministry leaders are angry that donors receive their appeals and yet don't give ("What is wrong with these people? Can't they see the value of what we're doing?"); these leaders are tuned in to themselves but not to their donors.

The most effective way to inspire a donor is to expose that donor to authentic changes happening in people's lives as a result of the ministry's work.

The most effective way to inspire a donor is to expose that donor to authentic changes happening in people's lives as a result of the ministry's work. I urge ministry staff members to get involved with the ministry so deeply that they have their own genuine stories to tell about the impact of the ministry in their lives. At a youth camp, I took visiting donors and prospects to the large rock where I had committed my life to Christ at 18 — and explained that down through the years, hundreds of teens have done exactly what I did in exactly the same spot. Many of those visitors were inspired to help build new buildings at that camp — visiting parents gave several thousand dollars in a single summer. A field rep-in-training accompanied me on some of these tours. As she began interacting with groups of donors herself, I heard her telling the same story. After a time I encouraged her to tell her own stories, from her heart. Problem was, she had never been involved in the camp experience. So I stopped her in her tracks. "I don't want you bringing any more donors out here till you've been in a cabin for a week working with a bunch

"I don't want you bringing any more donors out here till you've been in a cabin for a week working with a bunch of kids."

of kids." The rep howled. "That's not my thing!" she insisted. "I can't do that!" "Well," I replied, "You've got to." She argued and argued. I held firm. I scheduled her as a cabin counselor. On the appointed day, she called in sick. The next day when she showed up for work, I put her in the car and headed for camp — over her objections. I visited the camp the next day; she was miserable. At the end of the week I returned for a parents' meeting; the rep was transformed. She had spent the week with five girls; their hearts and lives had been intertwined. She was laughing and weeping and being wise and overjoyed. "I sat on your rock!" she cried. "I led a kid to Christ!" That field rep went on to raise thousands of dollars to enable students to have the camp experience — and she had her own stories to tell!

> *The individual who says "I can sell anything — selling is selling — been selling all my life" does not understand that this is not about "sales." This is about authentic life change.*

I don't recruit "super sales people" as ministry representatives. The individual who says "I can sell anything — selling is selling — been selling all my life" does not understand that this is not about "sales." This is about authentic life change. It is about the power of God at work in people. And it is about getting involved in the lives of the people whom God has called to support, to empower, to undergird this supernatural work. I am not looking for a super sales guy. I am looking for someone to sit on the rock, someone who wakes up in the morning with a genuine passion for the ministry.

I often quote a letter from the mother of a camper which begins, "What have you done to my son?" He had been transformed from a so-called "devil boy" to an angel, by the power of God's love — experienced at camp. The letter was so beautifully written that we contacted the woman; we found that she was a writer, and we began employing her to contact families who had been touched through camp experiences. She could relate, and she could write with genuine passion. We want anyone representing a ministry organization to have a natural passion for the mission — not just a job description which dictates that they will accomplish certain functions.

An acquaintance of mine has moved from years of inner-city ministry administration into fulltime major donor ministry, and in my judgment he is not a natural "fit" for the role — but he is one of the great storytellers ever to serve in inner-city ministry. His experiences flow out of him in wonderful, passionate, firsthand stories. As I trained him, I put him in a role-playing scenario; the other guy in the scene was playing the part of a belligerent prospective donor. The trainee responded gently to every salvo, and for every point he made, he was able to tell a great story. He will succeed because of this!

4. Be willing to change the way you think.

It's hard enough to identify our attitudes and concerns, and those of our staff, about fundraising — but the even more formidable challenge is to change these attitudes and concerns.

To create a new culture in your organization will require enormous commitment. Getting to the point of that commitment can be very difficult. It's hard work. It takes time. It requires a long-term commitment. (Everything about this model of ministry is slow! If I make an initial contact with a prospective major donor today, his best gift is probably still at least two years away.) There is no quick fix. Along the way, beloved traditions often have to go by the wayside. Some longtime employees have to move on. But the dividends are worth the pain, because your donors will sense your organization's thorough, genuine commitment to them. (The flip side: donors quickly sense hypocrisy, manipulation, and selfishness in a ministry organization. They know when they are simply being "used.")

> *Donors quickly sense hypocrisy, manipulation, and selfishness in a ministry organization. They know when they are simply being "used."*

Also, maintaining that commitment throughout the organization requires relentless vigilance. I helped an organization create a new culture some years ago. But three years ago, they ceased their schedule of occasional meetings and communications designed to reinforce the values of the new culture. Just recently, with the inevitable turnover of personnel, they are seeing the old "turf mentality" creep into the organization, primarily through the influence of new staff. It's time to begin again, reinforcing the foundations of the new culture. The fact is that creating a new culture isn't enough; you have to re-create the new culture continuously. For that to happen, someone in the organization has to have this priority on their mind every single day.

> *Creating a new culture isn't enough; you have to re-create the new culture continuously.*

An organization wanted to do a $7 million capital campaign. The board worked hard to raise enough money to hire us for a feasibility study. I interviewed

73

about 25 donors personally; we did another 300 phone surveys and about 600 mail surveys. Among the major donors, one consistent message came back: *I have the means, I have the passion — but I don't believe the board of directors can handle the money.* The organization had the potential to raise the money they needed for the campaign — but only if those who had arranged for the study were willing to step down.

> *It may even feel a bit infantile at first, but you have to start with the basic question, "Why are we here?" and build from there.*

Now I had to face the board with our report! But God helped us. At the end of my report, the board immediately moved to have us conduct a board assessment — to restore the confidence of the ministry's major donors. I deeply admired that group of leaders. They were more committed to the success of the mission of the organization than they were to their own position, status, or power. And one of the biggest donors, with the deepest concerns about the board, went on to enthusiastically chair the capital campaign!

5. Start at the beginning.

I list this point last because it must be the first and freshest idea of the process. To develop a new culture in your ministry organization, you must begin with the most basic fundamentals, training and leading your staff from the ground up. It may even feel a bit infantile at first, but you have to start with the basic question, "Why are we here?" and build from there.

A pilot leaving New York City and heading for London will totally miss the British Isles if his heading is *one degree off.*

To arrive at the destination of a healthy culture, start right.

I coached youth league basketball for 15 years. Every year, regardless of the history or experience level of the players on my team, I would begin the first practice session of the season by seating them all in a circle on the floor and holding up a basketball.

"This," I announced, "is a basketball."

I would then proceed to explain to them what a basketball is made of, how much rubber and how much leather, how air pressure impacts the flight of the basketball, what makes a basketball bounce, why a basketball spins off your fingertips. I would then move on to an explanation of the most basic concepts of the game of basketball. We would run the very simplest drills in that first practice session. It didn't matter if they were first graders or eighth graders; the beginning of the season was always the same.

Why? Because our players' basic understanding of the game was an essential building block to our team's success. We had to be sure that every individual was on the same page, working from the same list of definitions and perspectives and priorities. We also had to be sure that the most basic good habits were well understood and well established. A team of untalented players might never excel beyond the basics, but at the very least we would all have the basics in hand. And certainly even a very talented team would fall short of its potential if the players were not working together, completely agreed on the priorities and completely proficient in the basic skills of the game. I've won a great many trophies with mediocre teams that had learned to work together — and blown a great many tournaments with highly talented groups of players who had never gelled as a *team*.

In creating a healthy new culture within our ministry

organizations, we must ensure that the entire team is on the same page at the same time working toward the same goals. They need to see their roles as integrated and overlapping. They must not persist as a number of teams, each doing its own thing, but rather as one team, with each member contributing to the success of the whole. In basketball, I need Johnny to be as tuned to passing and assisting opportunities as he is to shooting opportunities. In ministry, I need the data entry clerk in the donor records office to be tuned to new movement, up or down, in a donor's giving. I want that clerk to call the field representative and give him a heads-up, so he can zero in on any significant change in that donor's life. The clerk and the rep are partners, fellow members of the team, both equally committed to ministering to that donor. Team play wins games. The organization wins, and — of at least equal importance, if not more — the donor wins.

CHAPTER 9

A Demographic of One

An organization asked us to help them find more major donors. I began by asking what they were doing with the donors they already had. Don't waste our time, they replied. We're getting everything out of our donors that we can.

But in most ministry organizations, we find that some of the best donors have already been led by God into the ministry family; they simply haven't been engaged in a relationship that opens the door for them to give more generously.

So where are you finding major donors now? I asked.

Well, we don't spend any of our own money finding major donors, they told

Some of the best donors have already been led by God into the ministry family; they simply haven't been engaged in a relationship that opens the door for them to give more generously.

me. We go to other organizations' major events and circulate among the attendees, talking about our ministry. Sometimes we find people interested in what we're doing, and we solicit major donations from them.

I was stunned. As diplomatically as I could, I suggested that this practice was unethical. The other organization was going to the expense of pulling together hundreds, perhaps thousands of donors and potential donors for their cause. And this ministry was deliberately using this event to attract donors to their own cause. Sure, they told me, some get upset with us — but you'd be amazed how many major donors to other causes also get interested in our cause!

I asked why they didn't produce their own events. We don't have time to do that kind of work, they insisted. We don't have the funding to organize those events. The fraudulence of their approach to major donors was completely lost on them.

Beyond the obvious ethical considerations, however, this practice ignored the potential major donors already hidden in their "general" donor file. We began looking at the ministry's own donor base, and I was able to quickly identify certain segments of the file containing donors who might have the potential to give major gifts. They weren't giving major gifts at the moment, but they were "waving" to the organization, signaling their potential through their giving quantities or frequencies. These donors were saying, in effect, "Why don't you come see me?" I suggested we visit these people, get to know them, inspire them with the vision of the organization, challenge them to give to more significant projects. The people attending other groups' major donor events were giving major gifts because *those organizations* were doing these very things!

This organization didn't understand the importance of giving individual donors a sense of being valued, and a connection to the ministry. The reason most of our donors don't give at their capacity is because their vision of the ministry is limited by the way we communicate with them. If we invest in engaging them, interacting with them personally, they have a chance to become inspired by the mission — and support it more generously.

The reason most of our donors don't give at their capacity is because their vision of the ministry is limited by the way we communicate with them.

This ministry's donors had a higher capacity for giving. They had potential. But they were not becoming major donors because the organization was not investing in relationship with them as individuals. They saw major donors as a demographic group, and other organizations' events as a way of tapping into that group. If we come to see donors as individuals, it radically changes the way we approach them.

* * *

I often ask participants in our seminars, *What is your philosophy of ministry to major donors?* A lot of people answer by talking about "relationship," but no one has ever responded by saying, "We look at each major donor as an individual, and figure out how to interact with each one uniquely." This, however, is the ideal — and it is the model of major donor ministry that our agency espouses. Ministry representatives who manage 300 major donors can't possibly operate according to such a model. If I am designing an individual marketing approach for each donor, I can only relate to 60 or 80 donors at a time — and then only if I'm truly fulltime.

Before the computer, there was no such thing as "demographics." Now we tend to see people in statistical groups; an individual is simply a reflection of a larger "segment" of the population. Those of us in ministry tend to think this way about our donors. And it's not all bad. There are "general" donors and "large" donors. There are "active" donors and "lapsed" donors. With unlimited money, an organization could invest in all of them equally. But with the real-world constraints of a limited budget, we have to invest appropriately.

We tend to see people in statistical groups; an individual is simply a reflection of a larger "segment" of the population.

Ideally, though, we want to treat each donor as an individual as much as possible. Even a general donor whom the organization can really only afford to interact with via the mail can in some cases be afforded the dignity of a letter which bears his own name, instead of "Dear Friend." We certainly want to do all we can to treat the individual as a unique person.

With major donors, where we can invest more resources appropriately, we can interact with each individual uniquely. But many ministry organizations drop this ball. They see a person with a certain income or net worth as qualified to support their mission. But a representative from the organization forming a personal relationship with that donor may well discover otherwise. When we just assume a

When we just assume a donor's potential, we violate not only the donor but also the integrity of our own organization.

80

donor's potential, we violate not only the donor but also the integrity of our own organization. I need to get to know a donor, minister to that individual, learn about that person's interests and passions, and discover over time where (or whether) his interests and passions intersect with the vision of my organization. That donor is most prone to give at his capacity when he realizes where his God-given interests coincide with our organization's mission.

To achieve this kind of understanding requires a serious commitment to the donor. It means not only an investment of time, but also total honesty in explaining and presenting our case for support. It means an absolute avoidance of high-pressure tactics. It requires undying loyalty to the donor's need to put their funds into projects and ministries that meet his or her criteria of interest.

What is God speaking to this donor's heart about his financial resources?

In other words, we need to make our appeals based not on what our organization is seeking, but on what the individual donor is seeking. Where is God leading this person? What is God speaking to this donor's heart about his financial resources?

Several years ago when I was raising funds for higher education, I got connected with a wealthy young man who was deeply committed to higher education. Based on my knowledge of the extremely generous contributions he had made to various other seminaries, I felt sure he had the capacity to give $100,000 or more to our organization's library-building campaign. I invested a lot of time and energy in my relationship with him. But I never really got to the key questions: Where is God leading you? What is God speaking to your heart? So after quite some time, when he asked to meet with me — and bring along one of our theology professors — I expected him to write that big check. As we ate and talked, I was mentally breaking ground on that library. What I didn't realize is that the prospective donor was dedicated to supporting schools espousing Reformed or "Covenant" theology, while the seminary was staffed with deeply committed Dispensationalists from Dallas Theological Seminary. The donor gave us $10,000 as a sort of "consolation prize." The theology professor was thrilled, but I was embarrassed — and I couldn't help but see it as a $90,000 error on my part. I had focused on the dollars instead of the donor's value system. I had failed to follow my own advice: *Know thy donor.* (On the way back to the office, I said to the theology professor, "We could be Covenant, couldn't we?" A few days later, my name came up at a faculty meeting. They were concerned that "Tim might compromise the theological integrity of the institution." "It was a JOKE!" I assured them. But I didn't feel very humorous.)

It's not really hard to find out how a person's heart is beating. But it's easy to miss — if you're thinking of the individual as part of a certain economic demographic segment instead of as a unique human being with likes and dislikes and passions and foibles and perspectives of his own.

It would have been easy for me to ask, "What kind of schools have you supported in the past?" It's not really hard to find out how a person's heart is beating. But it's easy to miss — if you're thinking of the individual as part of a certain economic demographic segment instead of as a unique human being with likes and dislikes and passions and foibles and perspectives of his own.

* * *

I worked with a ministry whose number one contributor felt that no one other than the president of the organization should ask him for money. I knew that I could never ask him for help for the ministry. I could work on the proposal; I could help the president prepare for the meeting — but I could never go to the donor's house. He was certainly in the "demographic" which would normally have led to my being personally involved. But we *knew our donor.* We sent the president to his house, and the president came home with the donations.

One donor to the organization had been giving major gifts for over four decades. We knew from experience that he would mercilessly grill the individual asking him for a contribution — but then he would give whatever was needed. The representative going to the donor's home always tried to stay upbeat and open during the encounter, but he always came home feeling discouraged, often sadly assuring the rest of us that he had failed. Yet within a few days, we would receive a check for $18,500 or $60,000 or whatever amount had been requested. We *knew our donor.* We were more concerned about the donor's preferences than our "donor program."

CHAPTER 10

What I Want to Know Is...

As we work with donors personally, in spite of the fact that each donor is a unique individual, we'll likely discover that a major donor or prospective major donor is asking certain internal questions, either spoken or unspoken, which we need to answer as part of our ongoing ministry to the donor. In many cases we need to see "through" to the actual issues on a donor's mind:

Donors are asking questions about your ministry's goals and objectives.

These are the "So what?" questions. Does your ministry intersect with the things I'm interested in? What difference is your ministry really making?

What difference is your ministry really making?

Donors are asking about the uniqueness of your ministry.

What are you doing that is not being done by anyone else? Why are you doing this? Why is this your mission? What

What are you doing that is not being done by anyone else?

compels you to do the things your ministry is doing?

Donors are asking about how much money your ministry needs to raise.

How big is the financial need? And how are you going to spend the money I give? Do you have a budget? What's the plan? Have you thought this through? Does it make sense to be spending the amount of money you're talking about on this project?

Donors are asking if you will be able to handle the donation wisely.

One donor gave nearly a third of a million dollars to a ministry organization. After a rocky year, representatives from the organization returned and asked for another contribution. "I didn't mind giving last year," the donor explained, "to get that project under way. But now you're asking me to correct your mistakes. Speaking as a businessman, I think you should just shut the project down." The organization came to us for advice. I suggested that the donor

How are you going to spend the money I give?

might actually give again, if he could see that the ministry was turning things around. We helped the organization revise the components of the project that were in disarray. Then we returned to the donor. He gave immediately, and generously. He saw a growing wisdom in the ministry's leaders.

Donors are asking about assessment and evaluation.

Will you be reporting back to me on the progress of the project you've asked me to support? When will it be done? How will you get back to me? (An important part of what gives a donor a sense of fulfillment is the *accomplishment* of the project.) How can you assure me that your reports will be accurate?

An important part of what gives a donor a sense of fulfillment is the accomplishment of the project.

The number one complaint we observe on the part of major donors is a ministry's failure to return with a report on the outcome of the investment the donor made in the organization. (Remember the youth-oriented ministry whose board chairman I advised to stop giving? In spite of his high position, he received so little information between annual requests for help that he felt completely out of the loop and ultimately abused.)

Donors want to know about the prior accomplishments of the ministry.

How has your ministry performed in similar situations in the past? They are very interested in your track record. Did you succeed in the past? Did you follow through on the things that you said you would do with the project?

Did you follow through on the things that you said you would do with the project?

We work with a unique ministry called Faith Comes By Hearing which records and distributes the New Testament on cassette tape in the languages of the world. We helped them mount a campaign to fund the recording of the remaining unrecorded "trade languages" — languages used by enormous overlapping people groups — which would make it possible to reach huge multitudes with the Gospel. One of the strongest arguments we were able to make for support of this campaign was the fact that Faith Comes By Hearing had already recorded nearly 50 languages. We could point to a certain amount of money required for the successful launch of a new language outreach. We could point to the organization's solid track record of assembling good recording teams, producing reliable "ministry product," and distributing tapes efficiently. A strong past is a strong foundation for funding the future.

A strong past is a strong foundation for funding the future.

The record of an organization's past also tells the donor that the organization has stayed on its intended mission for a period of time. Ministries with "mission drift" — switching gears and focusing on different priorities from time to time — don't inspire confidence in donors. (Still, many organizations drift. Their leader may be mercurial or entrepreneurial, seizing upon each new passion that strikes a chord in his heart. Each new warp of the organization's mission, however, means a re-building of the donor base.) A record of accomplishments assures the donor that the organization knows what it's about, and is likely to keep being about that same mission.

Ministries with "mission drift" — switching gears and focusing on different priorities from time to time — don't inspire confidence in donors.

Donors want to know about other financial supporters of the ministry.

What about your current donor constituency? How many donors do you currently have? What levels of support are they giving? Who serves on your board of directors? Do your board members give? If not, why not? What percentage of your budget is represented by board support? (A red flag goes up for a new major donor if a ministry has a great mission statement on paper but its own board members don't take an active role as donors.)

How to know whether an individual donor is asking any or all of these questions? Answer them in advance. Assume the information is desired, and offer it. You'll sense the donor latching on to the concepts of greatest importance to him.

> *How to know whether an individual donor is asking any or all of these questions? Answer them in advance.*

* * *

It is an inevitable side-effect of relational major donor ministry that an effective ministry rep will form close bonds with major donors — and if the rep leaves the employ of the organization, the donor is likely to follow him. This, however, is no reason for an organization to avoid forming relationships with donors! It is simply incentive for the organization to take good care of its reps. I urge organizations to establish excellent compensation programs for their representatives, linked to major contributions generated by their ministry. Some ministry leaders object. "Under such a plan, he could make more money than me!" My response is: *So what?* If your paycheck is so linked to your pride, you have a more important issue to deal with than the potential loss of a major donor. There should be no problem with a ministry representative making $150,000 if he is bringing millions of dollars into the organization, as long as the arrangement complies with Evangelical Council for Financial Accountability (ECFA) guidelines. (Also, with money flowing into the ministry, all executives and staff members have the potential to make more respectable salaries.)

CHAPTER 11

The Four Phases

How exactly should a ministry representative actually go about presenting the organization's case to a donor and asking for the donation?

Many ministry reps are impatient. They want to make the contact, present the case, "close the sale," collect the gift, and move on to the next donor. Others are too timid. They present the case, present the case, present the case — never quite sure about the "right moment" for asking.

After years of working with major donors, we have come to believe strongly in a four-phase approach to major donors: acknowledgment, trust building, presenting the case for support, and the ask. The sequence is important. Most significantly, these phases keep the donor's needs, interests, and values in view at all times. Let's look at each one, and investigate the timing and substance of each component.

Acknowledgment

The foundation of my relationship with a donor, like the foundation of my relationship with any friend, is what we call

Gratitude and appreciation are core to the relationship.

"acknowledgement." In my interactions with this person, I acknowledge his value as a human being by giving attention to his life, his activities, his opinions, his values. I don't just talk, talk, talk about myself and my ministry. I ask questions, I listen, I hear him out, I learn about him.

I also acknowledge a donor's generosity. Typically I will be interacting with an individual because he has already given a significant amount of money to my organization and we believe he has the potential to become a major donor. So an important part of my communication with this individual will be *affirmation*, acknowledging the role he has already played in the ministry, and thanking him for that. Gratitude and appreciation are core to the relationship.

Many people say, "You don't have to thank me." Thank them anyway. People need to be appreciated. They need, and they deserve, to have their generosity acknowledged. Thank a donor early, and often, and consistently. I call this "creating an atmosphere of appreciation." Your acknowledgment of their generosity should be "in the air," ever present. (I recommend that major donor ministers express thanks to a donor *within 24 hours* of receiving a gift. Drop a handwritten note; or at least shoot off an email. This sends the correct signal: "I noticed. You made a difference. And I am grateful!")

I also need to acknowledge that the donor's time is valuable. It's a sacrifice for a donor with significant resources to take time out for interaction with me, as a ministry rep.

When I'm sending a message of genuine thanks for the donor's time, I'm beginning to build credibility with him.

Acknowledgement is the crucial foundation on which any eventual request for funds must be built. One might say I must "earn the right" to present the case for support. If I have acknowledged the donor adequately, I can eventually present the case for support with confidence that I won't be violating the values of the donor, or unintentionally devaluing the donor.

Trust Building

A donor will not commit to a ministry where they have not established trust. The importance of this phase of major donor relationships cannot be overstated. No less than 80% of the time I spend with a donor will involve the trust-establishment process. If there is a single core to ministry-based fundraising, this is it. We don't hound, pressure, manipulate, or "emotionally inspire" a contribution from someone; we build trust, so that a contribution becomes the natural outflow of the relationship.

No less than 80% of the time I spend with a donor will involve the trust-establishment process. If there is a single core to ministry-based fundraising, this is it.

An effective representative of your ministry will be able to create confidence. The donor will come to have confidence in the integrity of the rep himself, and by extension in the integrity of the ministry organization.

Over time, as someone comes to trust me more, he will reveal more and more of his life to me. I will find myself learning about his thinking, discovering more about his value system, the personal details of his life, his involvement

93

in his church. It's typical of any growing friendship between Christians that the two individuals will swap stories about their families and churches. You make a new friend; you start learning, simply through conversation, about his work, his hobbies, his vacations. ("We ought to get our families together," I often hear from donors who are becoming my closer friends.) At some point, if an individual reveals his personal financial interests — if he talks freely about his investments or his tax bracket or other details of his financial life — he is demonstrating a significant level of trust in you. You don't typically talk about your assets with a stranger, an acquaintance, or even a casual friend. You talk about your assets with someone you trust.

I had a friend who, as it turned out, had several enormously valuable properties across the country. Some she had not visited in more than a year. Eventually, as our friendship developed, the day came when I could ask her, "Why don't you sell that place at Carmel, and put the money into ministry?" Obviously such a question could not be asked of someone who didn't trust me! But the fact that we could have such a conversation *comfortably* indicates that genuine trust had been established.

On the other hand, if I proceed to presenting a case for support and asking for a gift and the donor responds with a lot of skeptical, cynical questions, it is clear that I have misjudged; I have not established adequate trust with this person.

Presenting the Case for Support
The recognition of a donor's trust is a strong signal that he is ready to receive a presentation of the case for support of my ministry.

Many ministry representatives want a strict formula for this, but the nature of the presentation must grow out of our understanding of the individual donor's learning style. I need

94

to have a wide range of materials and types of presentations at my disposal, so that I can communicate effectively regardless of an individual donor's specific "wiring." How does this individual instinctively prefer to receive information? I have to stay flexible so I can communicate on the donor's unique wavelength.

I worked with a major donor years ago, a single medical professional who donated about 80% of his income to charities. He did not like to be asked for money at any time during the year; he would give only between Christmas and New Year's Eve, in order to determine his true financial position at year's end — and in order to be the "knight in shining armor" riding in on the white horse at the end of the year to help the damsel-in-distress ministry. I understood all of this about him — but what I did not understand was that he had an almost exclusively *visual* learning style. He was not a *text* guy, not a *charts and graphs* guy. He was artistic, expressive. Out to dinner with him one evening, I opened my laptop and showed him a seven-minute video prepared by my organization. He was mesmerized. "Show that to me again!" he said. We watched it start-to-finish *three times in a row*. He gave the largest contribution he had ever given to our ministry — over $50,000. We had gotten on his wavelength: *the visual wavelength*. Another major donor might not respond at all to a video; he might prefer charts and graphs. The individual donor might prefer conversation, or a letter, or a personal visit, or *no personal contact whatsoever!*

> *I need to have a wide range of materials and types of presentations at my disposal, so that I can communicate effectively regardless of an individual donor's specific "wiring."*

A donor began giving to one organization via the Internet. They were always odd amounts — odd numbers of dollars and odd numbers of cents. But when his contributions increased suddenly, I directed a ministry rep to call him, thank him, get to know him. "Why are you calling me?" he responded, sounding alarmed. "Don't ever call me again! I'll keep giving, but don't call me. And don't mail anything to me!" Emailing, he said, was okay. So the rep began communicating with the donor exclusively through email. Eventually she learned that the donor was a day trader, living and working in his home, and giving a fixed percentage of his earnings. But in spite of the rep's repeated entreaties, the idea of getting together personally was horrible to him. "I'm offensive to look at," he said, and he explained nothing more. He was getting enough information to make a decision. He loved to receive the photos that the rep emailed to him demonstrating the ministry in action, his investments at work. But he did not want to be seen. So we respected that. To this day, no one from the ministry has laid eyes on him — one of their biggest donors ever.

The message must come through in a medium that makes sense to the donor.

Present the case for support in a style that enables the specific donor, with his learning style, to say, "I get that!" Some donors prefer to receive digitized videos via email (my friend Chuck). Some prefer to have a casual conversation over lunch (my friend Alan). Some will only do this by phone (my friend Doug). Some prefer to be buried in audit numbers and information. ("I see here that this category jumped 12%; why?") The message must come through in a medium that makes sense to the donor.

* * *

I also need to make my presentation a natural expression of my own communication style. One ministry representative will be very comfortable with charts and graphs and grids; another would feel awkward making such a presentation. I should talk to my friend as if I'm *talking to my friend!*

It's also crucial for me to remember the values and passions that I have identified in this individual, and make my presentation in the context of those values and passions. To put it another way, I need to find the *intersection* of the donor's passions and the vision of my ministry.

Don't force a donor into a presentation. "Would you let me tell you about...?" is a great question to start with. Then, as I make my presentation, if the donor is truly ready to receive what I'm saying, there will be a connection. It will be evident if the donor isn't ready, in which case there is no shame in gently backing out of the conversation.

* * *

What should the presentation include, specifically? I believe in keeping it simple. Four essential components:

1. There's a problem in the world. (This is a mini-talk about whatever problem your ministry organization is dedicated to solving. Usually, this will track back directly to the mission statement of your ministry. A well-written mission statement will focus on the problem that your ministry addresses.)

2. There's a solution for this problem, and our organization is dedicated to that solution. (This is where you establish how your ministry accomplishes particular goals or meets the need addressed in your mission.)

3. There's a specific strategy for implementing the solution which we're focusing on right now. (This is about the project,

campaign, or aspect of the ministry which requires funding. What is the specific strategy, program or concept — *unique to your organization* — which meets the pressing need? This is where we answer the "So what?" question. The uniqueness of your ministry's strategy is crucial, because many major donors are frequently solicited for donations. It's essential that you make clear why *your organization* is the place for the donor to invest.)

The uniqueness of your ministry's strategy is crucial, because many major donors are frequently solicited for donations. It's essential that you make clear why your organization is the place for the donor to invest.

4. There's value in partnership. (What action on the part of the donor will help us solve the problem? Show the donor how he can be a partner in achieving the strategy, solving the problem, through a specific action on his part. This is the ultimate objective in our relationships with major donors. The relationship should lead us to a place where the donor sees how he can partner with us through his generosity.)

The Ask

Ultimately, you have to ask for money.

How do you transition from the presentation to the "ask"? Here are a few keys:

Make it personal, not "canned." If this is your friend, if he trusts you, if you've expressed the case for support as a friend-to-friend proposition, then the donor has absorbed enough information to process a specific request for help. Another aspect of keeping the ask "personal" is to frame the request for funds in the context of the donor's specific interests and passions.

Be sure the amount you are asking for is reasonable and appropriate for the donor. But aim for the "capacity" gift. What is this individual's greatest potential? Challenge the donor for the very "best" gift he can give.

(I was working on a ministry project which involved a number of $50,000 building units. I visited a wealthy man who had supported one of the ministry's staff members for years. He didn't give. Later I heard that his reaction to me had been quite negative: "Tim needs to get his act together. He shouldn't come asking me for $50,000 without knowing me better." I had been trying to leverage his long-time relationship with a member of our ministry staff — instead of forming the relationship myself, building trust, and earning the right to ask, and discerning correctly how much, and when, this guy could give.)

If this is your friend, if he trusts you, if you've expressed the case for support as a friend-to-friend proposition, then the donor has absorbed enough information to process a specific request for help.

How do I discern the amount to ask of a donor? I often ask the donor! A donor may have a $5,000 potential but only a $500 vision for what your ministry is doing. So it's important to challenge the donor for the *very best gift* he can give. Ask them to reach for the capacity gift.

This is where the relationship rubber meets the fundraising road. If the donor has any reservations about giving to your ministry, this is typically where those issues will come out! ("Let's say I give you the money; where do you connect with that many people in need?" Clearly I have not explained the case adequately — so I need to go back to the presentation. "I don't believe it could really cost a quarter-million dollars." Clearly I need to go back to building trust!)

But more often, you will find that donors are *more* able and *more* willing to give than you expected.

I consulted with a small youth ministry in the South. They believed they had "tapped out" their donors, but after many months of debate we convinced them to go out and actually have conversations with their donors. Just showing an interest in the donors, and asking them questions like "What inspired you to donate to us in the past?" led to an increase in response. Many of their one-time donors quickly became high-frequency donors. Their high-frequency donors moved up to mid-range giving. Their mid-range donors began to give at more significant levels. As they got to know their donors, their donors began to know them. Enthusiasm for giving to the mission followed naturally.

For the first time, their donors felt important; they felt they were valuable to the ministry. They felt as though the ministry genuinely cared about them.

In the course of this interaction, we made some interesting discoveries. We learned that the donors' giving capacity was on average much higher than the levels at which they had been giving. We also discovered that about 20% of their donors had major donor potential. Now, as their donors became better connected to the ministry, their passion easily drove their gifts to much higher levels. Within a year, we had identified one donor whose giving surpassed the entire previous year's ministry budget!

From then on, everything changed in that organization's approach to major donors. For the first time, their donors felt important; they felt they were valuable to the ministry. They felt as though the ministry genuinely cared about them.

When a donor makes this kind of connection to your ministry, they will begin to move up the ladder very quickly!

CHAPTER 12

Getting to the Ask

Here is language I often use when it seems like the right time to transition from presentation to ask:

"Dave, based on the information I've shared with you here, do you have any concerns about this project? Any questions I could answer? No? Would this be a good time to share with you what we're going to need financially? This is a $55,000 project. We're looking for three donors of $10,000 or more. Would you be willing to take one of those positions, to be one of those partners?" *Well, I need to talk to my wife; we need to pray about it.* "Awesome. I totally affirm that. When would be a good time for me to follow up with you about this? I don't want to bug you about it. You tell me." *Why don't you call me on Wednesday afternoon? I'll have this figured out by then.* "Cool. If you find that you have any other questions or concerns between now and then, just give me a call."

I trained a friend in major donor ministry, and by coincidence he ended up being the person in charge of money at my church. Years ago I helped establish a scholarship program to help young people in our church preparing for vocational ministry, and my wife and I pledged to give this year. Recently my friend called me. "We've got some applications to this program," he said in his gracious, low-key way, "and I notice that we haven't received anything from you yet this year." "Oh, man!" I replied. "I've been out of town so many weekends, I just forgot!" My friend was unfazed. "Great," he replied, "when should I follow up with you on that?"

Some people struggle with the ask, but not my friend. He and I were friends. He trusted that. He just asked me, almost with a shrug, about what I intended to do. I often ask trainees to imagine this scenario: you're the head of the evangelism committee for your church. You meet a guy who is clearly gifted in evangelism. Would you hesitate to ask him to serve on the evangelism team? No. Or you meet a guy who is clearly gifted in teaching. Would you hesitate to ask him to teach a class? No. But someone with the potential to give major gifts? Now, suddenly, I don't want to challenge him to exercise his gift of giving! Money changes everything.

But relationship greases the chute. If you're my friend, I can easily say, "Bill, can I come tell you about the project our organization is working on?" The friendship makes it natural. I don't need a script, because we're friends.

After I've worked with a major donor for a while, I actually tend to ask less often because *they ask me!* They get into the rhythm of the organization. They know that certain needs will occur at certain times. They become comfortable with their role. It's a casual but important thing. They call and say, "Tim, what's going on over there? It's about time for us to give." *Yes, it is!*

* * *

Consider these phrases, statements, and questions as part of your personal lexicon of donor relationships:

If I'm unsure about the donor's possible receptivity: "Does anybody in your circle of influence come to mind who might be interested in a project like this?" (If you are "with" me and you're willing to recommend your friends, you're probably ready to donate yourself. If not, maybe I need to go back to trust building, or the presentation of the case. The answer to this question defines *where the donor is on his personal journey*.)

If I'm unsure about the specific dollar amount that a donor might give — let the donor see the total need, and let the donor set the bar.

If I'm unsure about the specific dollar amount that a donor might give — let the donor see the total need, and let the donor set the bar: "Here's the project, here's what we're trying to do. It's going to cost $250,000. I'm going to need a donor to give $50,000, and four donors to give $25,000. I'll need ten donors to give $10,000 each. Now I know you have a vision for this. Where would you see yourself in this project? Do you see yourself as the top donor? Or somewhere else on the chart?" (In other words: this is the big picture, here are the pieces; which of these pieces do you think you could help with?) The donor will probably set his own bar by mentioning an amount. Not only does this tell me where to steer with him in this campaign, but it tells me I can probably *start* at that amount for the next campaign.

CHAPTER 13

How Many Hits, How Many Errors

Sad to say, in my many years of ministering to major donors, I have made quite a number of errors and learned quite a number of good lessons the hard way. In hopes that others can achieve an "end run" around my mistakes, I offer these pointers:

Allocate your time.

My friend Les Taylor, the former assistant chief of police in Tempe, Arizona, was an elder at the church where I was serving as executive pastor. The first time Les walked into my office at the church, he was astounded by my organizational system. It basically involved maximum use of the Post-It Note. I had little yellow rectangles stuck all over my work-space. Les immediately walked back out of my office, picked up a phone, placed a call, and returned to inform me that he had signed me up for a time management seminar. I was quite upset. I told him I didn't need to go to another time management seminar; it would just be a waste of my time. Les just smiled at me. Then he made it quite clear to me that I would attend this seminar, and I would pay close attention to everything that was taught. Over the next few days, Les followed up with reminder phone calls. On the appointed day, I drove to the downtown Phoenix location, walked into the hall, and plunked my bad attitude down in the back row.

But Les knew me, and he knew this seminar. The principles I learned that day have stayed with me all these years. One crucial concept: the wisdom of putting information in "a place your mind can trust." I didn't trust my memory to bring back the information I needed when I needed it, and I compensated with the yellow sticky notes. As a result of that seminar, I organized all of my contact information regarding the donors I was working with. I put all of my information in a single place, and established a calendar-alert system to make sure all the pertinent information surfaces on the right day at the right time. Today there are numerous such programs easily operated via computer or Palm Pilot. But a box of file cards and a Day-Timer can be rigged to work just as well. The bottom line is that your information about a donor needs to be put in "a place your mind can trust" — in other words, a substitute memory bank!

> *The bottom line is that your information about a donor needs to be put in "a place your mind can trust" — in other words, a substitute memory bank!*

Jim Holdman, a great systems trainer, also strongly influenced my career in ministry development. He introduced me to the "deferred calling system" several years ago. "Deferred calling" is necessary because "instant response" is so rare. Our donors are not waiting at home by their phones, or sitting in their offices, or standing at their mailboxes waiting for our calls and letters. Our donors are typically very busy people. They won't always be available when we call. They also won't necessarily respond positively to the initial appeal. We'll have to continue in relationship, and ask again later. All of this means that we as ministry representatives need a system of calendaring future call-backs. This is not simply for the sake of easing the stress, avoiding the strain of trying to remember when to do what with respect to which donor; it is also a means of serving our donors more fully. With simple but consistently followed systems, we can get connected and stay connected to donors more effectively.

(It is equally important that the organization's systems be in place and be effective. Sometimes I'll return to a major donor to request a second gift, only to have the donor advise me that he has never been receipted for his previous gift. This failure sends a terrible signal to the donor: it communicates that the organization is only using him for his money, that no one in the organization truly cares about him. And prompt receipting is only one among many systems that can help major donor ministers do their work effectively.)

Sometimes a system can solve a temperament problem. Chris Cole, the first person I ever trained in major donor ministry, succeeded because she not only embraced the philosophy of relationship, but she was also willing to become systematic about it. For example, she was anything but a morning person. She was a hard worker, but she would roll into the office at ten or eleven; it would be three or so in the afternoon before she became really productive. As her manager, of course, I wanted her in the office by 8:30 so she could be productive earlier in the day. So we adopted another Jim Holdman program

DONORS ARE PEOPLE TOO

called "Ten Before Ten" — ten tasks Chris was supposed to complete before ten each morning: check the database to see if we received a gift from any of your donors the day before; write thank-you notes to any donors whose gifts arrived yesterday; make phone calls to five new prospects; check your deferred calling schedule and set appointments; etc. Chris adopted the program and found that by ten in the morning, she was cooking. Ten Before Ten established a rhythm and a momentum for her workdays.

I still recommend Ten Before Ten. Plan ten activities or donor-related functions to be completed by 10 o'clock in the morning. A part-time worker or volunteer can adapt the numbers and the timing, but create some kind of timed agenda that will get you off to a strong start each day.

Keep in mind that when a donor agrees to meet with you, he is 80% likely to commit financially.

Ask for contributions consistently. Another way to say this is: Develop good "asking habits." Don't get lost in your relationship with a donor. Move toward the ask. Keep that goal in mind, no matter where you are on the relational track with that individual.

(A mentor of mine taught me that there were two basic truths about donors and fundraisers. First, people have a need to give. Second, we have a need to ask. Basically, our philosophy of asking is defined by what we believe about people.)

Ask with confidence. Anticipate success. Trust your ability to articulate the mission clearly, and ask fearlessly. Keep in mind that when a donor agrees to meet with you, he is 80% likely to commit financially. The face-to-face "ask" will impact the *size* of the gift because of the representative's passion for the cause.

Ask more often, and you'll gain confidence. Jim Fahringer discovered this. Jim is director of the Montrose Bible Conference in Montrose, Pennsylvania. He has spent the majority of his adult years at Montrose. I had the privilege of training Jim and mentoring him in the ministry of face-to-face fundraising. Jim is a man of great passion for the ministry God has given to him at MBC. He started there during college as a counselor, joined the staff, met his wife there, and has been director for several years. But Jim has never seen himself as a fundraiser. Because of the ministry's limited financial resources, Jim had to be the organization's initial field representative in addition to his other duties. Jim's first three fundraising calls were not only successful, but they went way beyond his expectations. As Jim received one commitment after another, a sense of confidence grew within him. He gradually developed the conviction that he was competent to do this type of work.

As the competence level grows in the fundraiser, the story gets a little simpler. As one of my mentors told me a long time ago, "Tim, a simpler story told with confidence will produce the desired financial results." I can make a complicated presentation, but a simple, streamlined communication is more effective.

> *I can make a complicated presentation, but a simple, streamlined communication is more effective.*

I also set a goal of at least four meaningful contacts with a major donor over the course of a year. If I'm in Chicago and you're in New England, it's probably not financially viable for me to visit you that many times. But it is viable for me to get on the phone with you. And based on the progress of my relationship with you, I am going to calculate how often — in those four contacts per year — I can reasonably ask you for money for my organization. In some relationships, once a year will be the limit. In other relationships, I may actually come to the point of being able to ask comfortably every time we talk. It depends on the donor.

You will not get a financial commitment on every first request. When you don't...

1.   Follow up with a personalized proposal designed with the individual in mind.
2.   Follow up with a handwritten note and e-mail.
3.   Follow up with a telephone call.

It's easy, but it's wrong, to interpret a first refusal as a firm "no." In all likelihood the donor just needs more information, more time to process the proposal, an opportunity to pray about it, or a conversation with his spouse. Don't assume he is saying no unless he tells you no. A donor often *sounds* as if he's saying no when he's actually saying *not now*. Follow up. (A handwritten note is still the most effective tool in donor relations.)

A donor often sounds as if he's saying no when he's actually saying not now.

I worked with a ministry organization that decided to plan a major event. One donor, whom I'll call Sam, was particularly excited about the idea and pledged a major contribution toward it if the organization would mount it. With the program largely mapped out, I visited the donor to access the contribution. "Well, I don't know," he waffled. "I'm not really sure this is my thing." I was confused, I told him. At breakfast several months ago, your enthusiasm gave birth to this idea. You inspired the organization to do this. "Well, I'll just have to pray about it," Sam replied.

It would have been easy for me to stalk away, angry and disillusioned, determined not to waste my time on this welcher. But I was in relationship with Sam. I knew him well. I knew how his mind tended to process, and how he tended to verbalize his thoughts. So I sensed that he was not actually saying no; he was actually saying *wait*.

So we proceeded on plans for the event. Meanwhile, I thought back through all of my previous interactions with Sam. I remembered that he had expressed concern about the organization's follow-up on attendees to past events. But we had worked hard on our follow-up programs in the interim; Sam just didn't know about them yet.

I went back to see him again. He was impressed. "I'll give you $25,000," he said. "But I want to see the follow-up on this next event before I give you any more."

We took his money. We produced the event. It was an enormous success, with 3,000 in attendance. We did the follow-up. We documented it all.

I went back to see Sam one more time. He wrote us a check for another $25,000.

I could have told myself that Sam was not committed to the ministry or the event. But Sam wasn't saying no. He just needed to be sure that his values were represented in the project, and he was wired to require consistent communication along those lines.

Some time later I was working with another ministry organization. One of the ministry reps returned quite discouraged from a donor visit. It turned out that he had been to see Sam, who was also interested in this organization's work. I asked the rep to describe the conversation with Sam. He gloomily did so. *He was rude, he was cold.* I smiled the smug smile of the insider. "I don't think he told you no," I offered. "Really?" the rep answered, puzzled.

Keep your eye on the donor. Remember, he needs your ministry more than you need his money.

Months passed. I ended up at lunch with Sam again, and asked about his encounter with the rep from the other ministry. "Those guys are doing something really important!" he said. He was positive. He was excited. But it was simply in his nature to process, analyze, ponder, discuss — and the rep would either be patient and tolerant, or he would give up too soon!

Don't lose sight of ministry in the life of the donor.

In any discussion of presentations, closings, and financial dividends, we can easily lose sight of the main focus of our activity. Keep your eye on the donor. Remember, he needs your ministry more than you need his money.

The key to all donor relations work is to keep *ministry* the primary focus in all of your dealings with your donors. Our focus will tend to drive to balance sheets, financial statements, and portfolios. But donors are people, and people have needs. People follow their passions.

Many of the donors you build a relationship with on behalf of your

Many of the donors you build a relationship with on behalf of your ministry will develop a closer relationship with you than they have with their own pastor.

ministry will develop a closer relationship with you than they have with their own pastor. Honor them with that kind of trust.

Don't be surprised when your meetings with a donor, your interest in his life, becomes a centerpiece of his world. Stay "locked in" on the focus of genuine significance in your relationships at all times. When this message of sincerity and genuineness in relationships connects with your donor, the transition to seeking financial support will be a natural one. Your personal relationship will grow out of the values that you share with the individual. Financial gifts will flow from the same values!

CHAPTER 14

Coming Back for More

As I teach the principles of major donor ministry across the country, I find certain questions coming up regularly. Here are several, along with answers we've found to be true:

Why are you so focused on keeping donors instead of getting donors? Isn't acquiring donors more important and more difficult than anything else? Donors are typically attracted to a particular ministry or case statement due to its uniqueness, the sense that this is something really special. In spite of the challenges to donor acquisition, our focus has to be grounded in donor *retention*. Our greatest impact with major donors will be seen in their long-term retention by our organization. If you are persuasive and passionate, a prospect will typically give that first gift (if for no other reason than to get rid of you). But the difference between the donor who gives a one-time gift and the donor who engages for a lifetime really boils down to personal relationships — and the systems that drive, connect, organize and maintain those relationships.

But the difference between the donor who gives a one-time gift and the donor who engages for a life-time really boils down to personal relationships.

Can anybody learn to do major donor ministry? We work with many ministry organizations in recruiting major donor ministry representatives. Certainly we want people with good personalities. We want the ministry to be represented by people with good "people skills," people who are highly relational. But at the end of the day, we have to nail down the answer to one key question: "Are you *called* to a *life of ministry to our donors?*" I admit that at times I have been wowed by the "super salesperson," the one with incredible sales experience and an infectious personality and spirit. But they have failed miserably in our ministries because of the lack of *calling*. To approach fundraising as a ministry of genuine relationship with your donors is to adopt a mindset which says: *"The donor really is more important than the dollar."*

How can a donor warm up to a friendship with someone who (they know full well) is a fundraising professional? I am more committed to the donor, to the relationship, to meeting the needs of that individual, than to raising money from that person. The skeptics say, "Tim, this doesn't work. The donors see through this as manipulation or deception. They know our pursuit of relationship is just to get them to give." Certainly this is true of someone whose ultimate motive is money! If, however, the motive is to allow God to lead you to relationships with people who have a genuine interest in your ministry, you can make that relationship genuine. If you have a sense of calling to see the Gospel improve people's lives, the donor senses that. He sees me not as a fundraiser, but as a friend.

Friendship is not established over a lunch or a cup of coffee. Friendship is developed through many levels of contact and experiences, and over *time*. Even though we both know that I'm a fundraiser, giving to my ministry becomes of little consequence to the donor when he experiences the ministry that I provide for him. It is natural for all of us to put our money where our passions are. When a donor discovers that his value system intersects with the mission of my ministry, it's a "given" that he will give! My greater concern needs to be about the fulfillment the donor experiences as a result of that giving.

> *Friendship is not established over a lunch or a cup of coffee. Friendship is developed through many levels of contact and experiences, and over time.*

If donors are manipulated, coerced, and pressured into giving merely out of our need or a sense of urgency, we cannot be assured of their long-term loyalty and commitment to what we do. Loyal, long-term donors are the result of healthy relationships, and requests for funds that flow out of those relationships.

Isn't it obvious to the donor that this is really just another way for the organization to make money? I want to see donors giving out of passion and experiencing real fulfillment. When a donor is experiencing fulfillment and joy in giving to my ministry, then I know he is giving with a sense of what God has inspired him to do. My greatest delight as a ministry-based fundraiser is seeing a donor reach for that "capacity gift" — not simply because of the size of the contribution, but because I know that this donor is following God, entering into the adventure of letting God guide him in the distribution of his resources.

> A philosophical commitment to "ministry first" with your donors will build a foundation for your fundraising efforts that will sustain your ministry for a long period of time. It is the basis for future success.

Does this approach to major donors require more time? Absolutely. The process of building significant friendships and relationships is a lifelong commitment. Ministry-based fundraising will not typically turn around an organization in a hurry. However, a philosophical commitment to "ministry first" with your donors will build a foundation for your fundraising efforts that will sustain your ministry for a long period of time. It is the basis for future success.

I find that rather than a donor's cynicism about the organization's motives, it's an over-zealous passion for the ministry that more often requires attention. I knew one major donor who grew so intense in his enthusiasm for a ministry that he nearly sold off a valuable collection that he had spent his entire adult life assembling, in order to donate the proceeds to the organization. It would have meant a huge amount of money for the ministry, but I intervened and counseled strongly against it. I felt the donor was out ahead of the organization. It seemed a sure thing to me that he would regret this emotional, spontaneous decision, sooner or later. Without realizing it, he was trying to compensate for years living far from God. *Pace yourself*, I urged him privately. If his loyalty to the organization could be moderated, he could be deeply fulfilled in his ministry of giving, the organization could benefit, and the relationship could be mutually rewarding over the long haul.

What do you do about relational major donor ministry if you come across a major donor whom you simply don't like? I look for someone in my organization who might be a better relational fit for this donor. I once dealt with a donor who was so competitive that I couldn't enjoy playing golf with him. But he also loved fishing — which I abhor — and another member of the ministry staff was a fisherman. I got them connected, and more or less breathed a sigh of relief.

The contributions kept flowing in from this donor. Some time later I checked back with the staff member. "How's that going?" I asked somewhat hesitantly. "Oh, we go fishing two or three times a month," he replied happily. Huh? "He's such a nice guy!" Are we talking about the same guy? As it turned out, the competitive golfer was miraculously transformed by the serenity of a lake. As a fisherman, he was a quiet, calm, reflective fellow.

A donor's loyalty to my ministry is one, perhaps the only, meaningful signal of the success of my ministry to that individual.

The staffer and the donor became fast friends, and our organization was able to continue in a mutually valuable relationship with the donor.

(On the other hand, if I don't like a donor and I can't find someone else to minister to him, then I have to be a grown up, deal with it, and minister to him anyway.)

* * *

Ultimately, each of these issues comes down to donor loyalty. A donor's loyalty to my ministry is one, perhaps the only, meaningful signal of the success of my ministry to that individual. Is this a friend for life? It's up to me. There's no reason a friendship can't span a lifetime — even if one of those two friends is a fundraiser!

CHAPTER 15

David the Fundraiser

Some resist the very idea of fundraising. I have often heard well-meaning Christians claim that fundraising is not biblical. This seems strange, when the Bible talks more often about money than about heaven or hell! Rarely does the person who objects to fundraising also object to the concept of asking for help in any other realm of life. It's just that the subject of money makes people nervous; the prospect of having to part with any portion of their financial resources is painful. The financial is often the final realm to be turned over to God in any believer's life.

People tend to become even more agitated when discussing major donors. They complain about the idea of giving preferential treatment to individuals in a donor base who have the capacity to give larger sums of money than others. How can we reconcile this with the way in which we relate to our other donors?

Let's look squarely at the Word of God and see what several models indicate.

Leadership

In 1 Chronicles 22, David gives instructions to his son Solomon about building the Temple to house the Ark of the Covenant. He plans to hand over the leadership of the project to Solomon, and he admits that his boy is young and inexperienced. So David is covering his bases in advance, to ensure the success of the program.

Typically we do not fail in our major donor relationships as a result of a poor mission or vision statement. We do not fail because we lack passion and purpose. We fail because we do not lead.

Most development efforts with major donors break down as a result of leadership. Typically we do not fail in our major donor relationships as a result of a poor mission or vision statement. We do not fail because we lack passion and purpose. We fail because we do not lead. Many ministries today are struggling due to the failure of a president, executive director, or even a development officer who is not leading others.

And it is crucial for our ministry leaders to lead in the realm of major donor ministry. In 1 Chronicles 22, David definitely goes there. David gives before he asks. Then he speaks of men with *special* talents and gifts (verse 15) who can provide resources and services *that others cannot*. He places a *priority* on these individuals. Do they receive greater favor in the eyes of God? No. Do they possess some special secret to a deeper spirituality? Absolutely not. But they are singled out, and asked to serve in a special way, because of their unique capabilities for the sake of the kingdom. Like major donors, they have a gift and ability to do something beyond the ordinary.

Does David hem and haw? No. He exhorts them to take financial responsibility. He "ordered all the leaders of Israel to help his son Solomon" (verse 17).

David was a true leader. A ministry needs a leader who is committed, passionate, and willing to take the heat when necessary, in order to inspire and compel others to follow his God-given passion.

As a high school student 30 years ago, I heard a speaker at a camp challenging me to "light my soul on fire." "Tim, if you can get more passion and purpose behind what you believe in," he said, "you can impact your high school for the kingdom." He inspired me. I remember going to school that next fall and praying, "God, light me on fire, and compel others to come watch me burn for you!" That passion to see teenagers come to Christ and in turn influence their school campuses still burns within me today. As that speaker led me, we need to lead others. Leaders need to lead.

Example

In I Chronicles 29, David goes on to show how some giving generously can set an example for others:

"Then the leaders of families, the officers of the tribes of Israel, the commanders of thousands and commanders of hundreds, and the officials in charge of the king's work gave willingly" (verse 6).

Here David is leading his people into a major capital project. He identifies the best prospects first. He finds not the only prospects, but the best prospects to leverage his resources in time to complete the project that God has laid on his heart.

David goes public. David has the leadership — the wealthy — give publicly as an example to the rest of the people. In turn they rejoiced in giving.

David now speaks to the "great men of Israel." He instructs them to contribute towards the building of the temple. He invokes a very familiar New Testament charge to the Church: "provoke one another to good works" (Hebrews 10:24). The principle here is to not be satisfied with only doing good things ourselves, but to influence others, to draw them into good works themselves.

> *The principle here is to not be satisfied with only doing good things ourselves, but to influence others, to draw them into good works themselves.*

Example is essential. I am always sadly amazed when I meet fundraisers who do not give personally to the projects they are raising funds for. I recall one ministry I was involved with. A staff member challenged me angrily because he was not receiving the organization's direct mail communications. I quietly informed him that those were communications we mailed out to our *donors*. The best way to get on that mailing list was to become a *donor*. He didn't ask me any further questions.

David goes beyond example, to enthusiasm. He now attempts to get the people as excited as he is about this project (verse 5). He talks about having your "hands filled." When you engage with God in giving and service, your hands will be full. We're called

> *When you engage with God in giving and service, your hands will be full.*

not to stop with our intimate following of Jesus, but to serve Him out in the open, to serve Him liberally with all that we have.

"Now, who is willing to consecrate himself today to the

Lord?" he asks in verse 5.

David is striving to compel a group of people who are uniquely gifted — gifted to give generously. David even gives himself to rejoicing. Likewise, at the end of our lives, our desire as ministers to major donors should be to look back and see that we inspired people to desire more out of God, and to get more out of the resources God blessed them with.

The result of David's approach? People gave (verse 7)! They rejoiced and gave willingly. They were fulfilled. They were glad to honor God out of their substance.

Joy

In 1 Chronicles 29:16-19 we see the flow of joyful giving. God honors us when we give. This isn't just an intellectual benefit. It *feels* good. It generates joy! It was David's *pleasure* to know that God was pleased with what he had done in His name.

He now comes to God and offers a prayer that his son will hold fast to the vision.

> *God honors us when we give. This isn't just an intellectual benefit. It feels good. It generates joy!*

Stewardship

In 1 Timothy 6, Paul addresses people who want to be wealthy. A few verses later, he talks about those who already are. Paul's consistent message about the stewardship of God-given resources, financial or otherwise: Examine your attitude.

"Command those who are rich in this present world not to be arrogant nor to put their hope in wealth," he says in verse 17.

What should their attitude be? He recommends that they

place their hope in God, not in their wealth.

"Command them to do good," he continues, "to be rich in good deeds, and to be generous and willing to share. In this way they will lay up treasure for themselves as a firm foundation for the coming age, so that they may take hold of the life that is truly life."

On the strength of God's Word, we challenge major donors to step up and give to God's work in major ways. We do it because it is God's design. It is a spiritual exercise. It is good for the donor. Along the way, it is good for the ministry.

The Scriptures themselves call on major donors to give. The wealthy are repeatedly challenged to be quick to give. Be always ready to share what they have with others. Those who are "rich" are to not have their sights set on their "riches"; they are called to put their hope in Christ who "richly provides."

* * *

On the strength of God's Word, we challenge major donors to step up and give to God's work in major ways. We do it because it is God's design. It is a spiritual exercise. It is good for the donor. Along the way, it is good for the ministry.

No book, of course, can address the application of every principle in detail as it relates to any given organization. So we urge you to contact us. Let's dialogue about your ministry. If we can help you minister to your major donors, we would welcome the opportunity.

Contact Tim Smith via tsmith@servantheart.com.